Islamic Ideals

(English)
Islamic Ideals

PROF.A.NABEESATHU BEEVI
First Edition : May 2014
Cover : Manoj Majeed
Rights Reserved : Prof. A. Nabeesathu Beevi

Islamic Ideals
(study)

Prof. A. Nabeesathu Beevi

Prof. A. Nabeesathu Beevi

Born on Feb 14th 1947 in Kunnumpuram House, Madavoor-Pallickal, in the District of Thiruvananthapuram. I have studied at Pallikal Government Primary School until Fifth standard. High school education was at Pakalkuri Government High School. In 1962 as the first Muslim girl I have passed SSLC from Pallickal - Panchayath. After passing M.A. History from the University of Kerala with first class started teaching career at Government Women's college Thiruvananthapuram. After meritorious service in different Government colleges retired from service in the year 2002. I am lucky to be the first Muslim M.A. holder and Govt: College Professor in Pallickal- Panchayath.

My father and mother died respectively in the years 1994 and 2000. My brother Sainulabdin is a retired Sales Tax Inspector and sister Nazeera Beevi is a retired Government high school teacher. My husband is practicing as an advocate at the District Court Vanchiyoor Thiruvananthapuram. Only son Manoj Majeed is working in U S A and daughter also lives in Texas, U.S.A. with family. I have visited Canada, U.S.A, UAE and KSA and got the opportunity to visit the wonders of the world - Niagara Waterfall, Laurel Caves, Golden Gate Bridge, Zero Gravity Point and Silicon Valley Hills, Hollywood Studio, Empire State Building, C.N.Tower, Merilyn Manroe Tower and Burge Khalifa Tower.

Address:
Kareema,
House No 50,
N.P.P.Nagar Lane-2,
Peroorkada, Trivandrum - 695 005
Phone: 04712432246 mob: 9656261648.
E-mail:nabeesu_majeed@yahoo.co.in

Preface

When each religion is subjected to study and assess its efficiency using the terms of evolution of Human race, it would become clear that there is no powerful and energetic prediction like that of Mohammed (S.A.). But now we find not the holy words of Mohammad, but a completely changed one. It seems to have become another thing.

The basic factors like Thauheed Jihad and study of Qur'an have been mistaken. The philosophical and divine discussions of Thauheed has become impracticable and out of use. It has been misinterpreted as Terrorism, though it is intended to persuade man to do good to the people. Qur'an which shed the light of knowledge in a society deeply plunged in ignorance and darkness, is now wholly forgotten. The prayer book has been brought from the graveyard to the city and instead Qur'an was brought to the dead. This cunning tactics got victory. Qur'an has been snatched from the students and kept in the shelf. And instead Physics was given for studies. Thus Qur'an disappeared from the minds of man. The society as a whole became a scene of vulgarity.

A redemption from this is possible only when Qur'an is brought back to city and study it deeply. Those who read and learn it would come close to Allah. They experience that He talks and gives orders to them.

My motto was to write a small book with vast ideas. I have tried to make it simple. Muslims and other people can understand it. The ignorance and misunderstanding about Islamic ideology would disappear. The religious practices and faith would become very clear. It is hoped that this text would help to some extent to remove the mistaken belief that Islam is the origin of Terrorism.

The text deals with the faithful practices of the Muslims, Qur'an, Islamic rules, social-family –married life, the role of women, Polygamy and backwardness of Muslim. It is hoped that it would be beneficial to all people.

I express my heart- felt thanks to prof. P. A. Sahid who corrected the mistakes, Prof: Jadeeda, K. T. Kamaludeen M.A. M.Ed. LLB, M.Phil, Academician and Curriculum Developer. My sincere thanks goes to Maulavi Jamaludeen Mankada, Ex.Imam Juma Masjid Palayam Thiruvananthapuram who wrote introduction to the book and Janab Hafiz Mohammad Shafi Khasimi Imam Peroorkada Juma Masjids(2009-2010), who wrote valuable comments and suggestions about the book. I express my thanks to Prof. M. Sainudeen Head of Arabic Department University College Thiruvananthapuram who wrote a note of comment about the book and Janab Shahul Hameed for helping me in translation. Last but not least I express my sincere gratitude to S.Sundar raj who did the DTP work very sincerely. I pray to Allah the Omnipotent, to give rewards to all who helped me in this attempt.

It is requested that mistakes if any in the text may be pointed out. I pray to Allah to accept it as a noble act and give me reward.

Prof. A. Nabeesathu Beevi

Introduction

An era has passed by in Islamic Society. A period of negation of education and inactivity of Muslim women has disappeared. This period of conservatism and priesthood was actually drawing back Islamic society to old days. It caused great misery in the case of women. It had a great tradition of Ayesha Beevi (Ra) and such reputed women who led the Islamic society with strong determination and courage. Things as such the above said misery made a shock to the unity of women.

As the result of the interference of leaders of Renaissance and movements great awakening took place. Now Muslim sisters are found active and energetic in the fields of education and charitable activities. Their social interference is in every walk of life. Noteworthy contributions have been made by them by translating Qur'an and writing books on basic subjects and reacting to social movements in the light of Islamic views.

The attempt of the writer deserves to be encouraged. She tries to analyze Islamic ideas in the light of the knowledge she acquired by profound reading and studies. It would be beneficial to all who wish to know and understand Islam. This book has sixteen chapters. Worshipping, idealistic and performing zones of Islam have been dealt with in this book. Special emphasis has been given to the subjects, Islamic Family life, Marriage, Divorce, Polygamy and Status of women. Sachar Committee Report has been attached at the end of the text. As the attempt of a sister the work of Prof.A.Nabeesathu Beevi's entitled 'Islamic Ideals' should be approved and encouraged. Let the Omnipotent Lord of the Universe accept this humble work.

With prayer

Trivandrum,
10-12-2010

Maulavi Jamaludeen Mankada
Imam Pala yam Juma Masjid

A statement

I am proud and happy to announce a truth. The present time moves through a period of ups and downs in material prosperity and achievements. The attempt of Prof. A. Nabeesathu Beevi to educate the common people about the exhortations of Allah, is a noteworthy contribution. The contents in the book are the results of deep and wide studies of Qur'an.

This book is an answer to some extent to the challenges and criticisms made by the outsiders and the supporters of religion. It may be due to either their ignorance or selfish motives. The book may be subjected to a wide and detailed study by readers and they should show craze to copy it in their life. Let this great and humble work may be accepted by Allah as a noble act!

Hafiz Mohammad Shafi Khasimi
Imam Peroorkada Juma Masjid.

A note of comment

(A second reading of eternal Islamic Ideals)

There are many studies on the divine religion Islam in Malayalam. But writings of women are very rare in it.

The text 'Islamic Ideals' written by Prof. A. Nabeesathu Beevi is a noteworthy work as intelligent analysis of God created religion Islam on the basis of religious ideals of religions in general. In that aspect this book stands as a remarkable contribution.

Islam has imbibed the all the true idealistic views of God's revelation from the beginning of man, has survived all the limitations of time, nation and race. It's ideas and ideals are quite safe in monotheism. The beliefs and practices of Islam are good enough to keep up high values.

This text which introduces the forms of worshipping, practices and philosophical discussions are capable of creating awareness in the minds of people. The systems of marriage, technical words in the Islamic law social and economic transactions are analyzed in the book.

The social backwardness of Indian Muslims, their issues and solutions have been discussed brilliantly in the book. Not only that it can be called a hand book which contains ideas and suggestions for social progress of Muslims in India. In brief it would enable a second reading of the true and eternal ideals of Islam.

Thiruvananthapuram,
29-12-2010

Prof. M. Sainudeen
Head Department of Arabic
University College

Contents

Chapter 1
Islam

Religions and religious teachers came in to being as an initiative for renovation. All religious visionaries have become restless due to the decayed faith around them. No doubt their teachings were intended to make social renewal easy and possible. If Shri Buddha and Mahavira attained knowledge through strenuous meditation, Mohammed (S.A.) and other Prophets got their religious views through revelation. These people had something in common. Being discontented with the surroundings, they showed intense desire to reform it.

Each religious tradition seems to be emphasizing certain values—Hinduism in the result of Karma, Buddhism in Ahimsa, Christianity in love, mercy and Islam in equality and justice All these values are complement each other. A combination of these makes the writings of religion. If one of these is found lacking, worldly life will become useless because these are necessary values for life. These values were the weapons in the hands of visionaries and religious Prophets for building a society, with motives and relavance. It is quite unfortunate that religious followers have rejected these values. Instead of that certain practices have been accepted. People who took up the leadership of religions had selfish interests. Such people separated religious rituals from ultimate aim and so they became mere mechanical force. Rituals and practices should be combined with the ultimate ideology and then only devotion and spiritual values will be perfect. Analysis of Islamic principles becomes relevant in this context.

The term Islam means surrender to the Cosmic Creator. Islam and Salam are interrelated. The word Islam is from the root 'As lama'. It means yield or dedicate. Salam means peace or quietness. That means perfectly peaceful or the origin of peace. 'Assalamu Alaikum' a salutation means let there be peace for you. All the religions have this sort of salutations. "If any one bows his face to the Allah and does virtuous deeds, the reward is in Allah for them nothing to fear. They need not be worried" (H.Q.2:112).

Islam means Qur'anic message. It is a creative religion based on equality and fraternity. It means surrender in the high state of identity and obedience to the laws between man and nature. "surely the acceptable religion in Allah is Islam"(H.Q.19:3). Islam calls for the unity of all religions and tells Muslims to accept it. When we consider the principles of Islam, what we call Muslims around us, are not real Muslims. Devoted Muslims should practice its principles.

All the religions in the world are known by the name of founders. But Islam exists as a world religion. As the names indicate, Christianity, Buddhism, Jainism, Zoroastrianism and Hinduism are separate. But Islam is not founded by an individual or meant for a particular sect. An invisible hand is always helping him in all the miserable stages. To do the will of God becomes his ideal of life. In this stage the Creator appears to be very close to him. The Creator says so "I am more close to him than his nerves" (H.Q.50:17). By the words and addresses of the Creator he becomes blessed. "Today I give you your religion perfect and my blessings in you are completed and I am satisfied Islam as your religion" (H.Q.5:3). This word in Qur'an stresses that religion has attained its perfection in Islam. The meaning of the word Islam is a 'perfect state.' Islam means ultimate obedience. It deserves the state of Moksha, by sacrifice not in words but in acts, surrendering to the Creator. In this state all noble qualities are blended in the man.

Undoubtedly Islam is a system. A right religion should reflect nature. It has the charm of nature. The fundamental message of each religion should come from its basic texts. If so the basic text of Islam is Qur'an. Qur'an is the last Vedic Text from God. It is impossible to gather knowledge about the Creator in a short span of time. It is like taking a handful of water from an Ocean. Qur'an says "The words of Allah cannot be written fully, even if all the trees in the world are pen, Oceans ink and another seven Oceans encourage it the words of Allah would not be exhausted. Indeed, Allah is Exalted in Might and wise" (H.Q.31:27). The fundamental theory is to believe in his identity, oneness, power and sovereignty and accept his Prophets and their advice. To establish God's supreme power and man's fraternity and to mould humanity as one race is the aim. The aim of Islam is to lead the people along the path of real joy and fortune and to attract them to the Creator to regain purity of life and to make them understand nature reasonably. Due to fear and blind beliefs in the secrets of nature man worships nature and even kills himself. The aim of Islamic religion is make the followers in the way of the Creator. Necessary guide lines have been given to it for the growth and development in every stage from the beginning till the end of humanity. Many Prophets have been sent to the world. There is no basic difference in the teachings and exhortations of these men. All those people taught nothing but Islam Just like the Ten Commandments of Jews and Christians, the Four Aria-Truths of Buddhism, Eight fold paths, the Three Jewels of Jainism, the five practices and Six Faith are the foundation stones of Islam. Ahimsa, the basic principle of Buddhism, Karma the basic principle of Hinduism, Love, Equality and Justice of Christianity are joined and blended all through the laws of Qur'an. Islam recognizes all religions given by God, in its origin all these were Islam. Qur'an claims: the supporters of each religion sent by Allah are Muslims by faith and morality. But now the terms Islam and Muslim are used to refer to the religion and followers of the religion of Last Prophet because religion becomes universal and perfect only with the Prophet. Qur'an declares that there is no humanity which has not been educated By God. By the encroachment of man all the guide lines and advice given time to time lost its original purity and underwent changes. Thus they got separated. The essence is the same in original form. It is centered round the one eternal Truth. The cosmic guardian is Allah. He is omnipotent, One and guardian of all. Universe is not Allah. But it is made and glorified by Him. It is being protected and he makes it survive. Galaxy of the universe is one, humanity is one, the creator is one and the religion of the Creator is one. No need for many religions to one human race. Though there are peripheral differences the basic laws are the same.

One faith, one order of practices, one Holy Text, One Human race, is the characteristics of Islam. The base of the Islamic society which obeys and worships the Creator being bound by the same laws and disciplined is the unity of faith of the individuals of Islamic society. The society of good people is always good. So Holy Qur'an addresses the followers as "A noble sect resurrected for the people" (H.Q.3:11). God's message reverberated in the Arabia desert is Islam itself the message given through Mohammad (S.A.) was the perfection and end of the message given by God through Prophets from time immemorial.

"Today I make your religion perfect and satisfied Islam as your religion" (H.Q.5:3).

The fundamental theory of Islam is to believe in the identity of Oneness, Powers and Sovereignty and accept His Prophets and their exhortations of the Creator. Thus establish God's sovereignty and fraternity of man and humanity in to one race. That is the aim. The people who had been worshipping Natural powers because of fear and even sacrificing man himself were attracted to the Creator and made them understand Nature reasonably by Islam .By regaining purity, people are led to all the fortunes of life.

The aim of Islamic religion is to make the people travel on the track of the Creator by giving guidance and advice in all the stages of its growth from the beginning till it lasts. Many Prophets have been sent to the world. All of them taught nothing but Islam. All their advice and guidelines were not different basically.

Like the Ten Commandments of Jews and Christians the Four Truths and Eight fold Paths of Buddhism and Three Jewels of Jainism, the foundation of Islam is its five daily Namaskar and Six Faith. The basic principle of Ahimsa of Buddhism, the Karma theory of Hinduism Love, Equality and Justice of Christianity, are found blended and merged throughout the laws of Qur'an.

Islam accepts all God sent religions. All these were in the beginning Islam, claims Qur'an. The followers sent by Allah of each religion, were Muslims by faith. Still the words Islam and Muslim represent the religion of the Last Prophet and His followers. Because religion becomes universal and perfect only with the mission of the Last Prophet. There is no humanity which has not received divine exhortation, Qur'an declares. These guide lines advised in different periods and countries, lost its initial purity by man's encroachment and under went many changes. As the result they became entirely different .In the root form it is the same. It is centered round the One Truth. The Lord of the Universe is Allah One, Omnipresent and Omnipotent. Universe is not Allah .But it is He who Created and glorified it. It is He protects it. The Universe exists because of Him.

The array of the Universe is the same .Humanity is one .The Creator of the Universe is one. His religion too is one .No need of many religions to a people. Though there were differences in detailed aspects they were one in spirit.

Islam imagines a society of equals with one faith one system of Practice One Text and one Society. Being bound by one Law and self disciplined we obey and worship the Creator. The unity of faith of the Islamic society is the unity of individuals in it. Society of good people will be good. So Holy Qur'an speaks about Islamic followers, "A noble society resurrected for the people" (H.Q.3:110).

The divine message reverberated in the deserts of Arabia in the seventh century is that of Islam. The message given through the Prophet was the perfection and end. "I hereby perfect and complete your religion I give it you as satisfied." (H.Q.5:3). That message is not to be changed according to time and country. It will remain until the end of the universe and survive all the laws of the world. If this knowledge from God made perfect through the Prophet could guide the people in between the fourteenth centuries it if it can govern people of all ages and countries, it is sure that it will remain a guideline till the last day. It is not a spiritual system of life that advises to keep away from worldly life and sit in meditation and prayer for getting salvation. It touches all the aspects of human life. It gives a proper perspective to the personal and social aims of man. It contains in itself a perfect code of theory to make man disciplined and spiritualized. Islam calls for revealing the visible and invisible truth. By mind, word, or act, and do accordingly. All the rituals of man are controlled in its limits. It does not enforce laws, but advises him to think and accept.

The original records are Allah, (The Creator) His angels, His Texts, His Prophets, Life in the other world, Belief that good and evil are decided from the Creator.

Islamic- deeds exists on the base of five orders of worshipping. These approve and declare the Oneness of Allah and the prophet-hood of Mohammed (S.A.) do Namaskar, give zakat (Compulsory charity) practice Vow in the month of Ramzan and do Hajj if possible.

Chapter 2
Iman or True faith

Revelation the pure form of knowledge should be assimilated through Iman. Iman (Faith) is a must for acquiring knowledge. Growth in science and urbanization improves our faith in the deeds of other people. So faith should never be tied up with spirituality, it should spread all the parts of mundane life. 'Knowledge is soul. Ignorance is darkness and death' (Hades). It is not a mere simile, but a scientific truth.

There should be Karma after Knowledge. That means real knowledge becomes right Karma and gives real result. Qur'an says more than fifty times that knowledge should follow Karma. Any act, however silly it is, should give an existing result. Qur'an says," If any one does an atom of goodness. He should see that; if any one does an atom of evil, He should see that too"(H.Q.9:7,8).The three principles of Islam Faith, Knowledge and Karma, three Jewels of Jainism, Faith, Right Knowledge and Right Karma are similar.

Iman is not mere keeping a faith, but practicing it through Karma. When we study about millions of cosmos and ask what is beyond it we are convinced that our knowledge is very silly. We understand that there is more to know about the mysteries of the Universe and the truth is yonder. If man has to understand his place, duties and his qualities in the Universe, other methods become essential. Divine revelation is a means to save man from his helpless condition and give him basic knowledge through Prophets. Divine messages had originated with the origin of man and given to humanity in all periods Believe in strongly in certain visible and invisible cosmic realities and practice it through life, are included in Iman.

Iman reaches perfection when it comes from the inner mind, grows and identifies with the mind and the soul. The tongue utters it. It is reflected in every movement of man. It is also reflected in all the deeds of man. Iman releases mind from artificial, physical and contextual slaveries. Iman attains perfection as dedication to Allah. It points out the high state of mental culture. It does not practice rituals mechanically. It fills the mind with the light of faith and makes changes and surrenders everything to Allah. Mind attains peace by thinking of God. Qur'an says "O Soul that attained peace, you return to your Guardian as contended and satisfied" (H.Q.89:2728).

One who accepts Iman is 'Muamin or true believer. Muamin has been moving away from sin. However if he feels sense of fear, he repents and seeks shelter in the Creator. Sins done consciously make scratches in Iman. These scratches are more painful to the believer than physical tortures. "True believers are those that feel fear in mind when speak about Allah and faith increases when read His words" (H.Q.8:2).The basic theory of Iman is strong faith in six factors like, Allah Malakkukal or Angels, Vedic Texts, Prophets, Last day, and the base of good and evil. Like wise the basic expressions of it are Prophethood of Mohammad (S.A.) oneness of God Namaskar compulsory charity Vow and Hajj. If Iman is to become perfect, strict approval and obedience to the commandments of the Creator are inevitable.

Chapter 3
Allah

The first and the foremost factor of I man's foundation stones is faith in Allah. No word with wider meaning has been used as the name of the Creator. So Allah deserves special study in the light of Holy Qur'an. He is a great force that creates, protects and controls not only the Earth, a people and a country, but it creates, protects and controls each and every thing in the universe. He is the Creator of all galaxies of the universe. His creative and destructive powers are only an atom comparing to his supreme powers. He is infinite and endless. He is beyond time. He is Omnipresent, Omnipotent and all knowing. He cannot be looked upon in terms of physical forms. All Cosmic activities are done by His will. He is self born and non-dual. "Say, he is Allah, one. He is the base of everything. No child is born to him. He is not the child of any one. None is equal to him" 112:1-4). By all means we recognize complete dependence to Allah and pray in words. And also pray for showing noble path in life. A true believer renews his remembrance to God directly to Allah through Namaskar. As far as a Muamin (True believer) his Iman is a door of virtuous deeds and an invincible fortress to evil deeds. So a Muamin should be pure of mind word and deeds. Virtuous deeds are unavoidable for the perfection of Iman and so we are exhorted about Karma. There is nothing as precious as true faith. They deserve Heaven. Holy Qur'an says; "If any one has done noble deeds as a true believer, whether a man or a woman, they will enter Heaven. Not even an atom of injustice should be shown to them" (H.Q.4:124).

Islam does not permit renunciation. Man is permitted to enjoy all fortunes given by God in certain limits. It should never be selfish. It should be done by fulfilling his loyalty to the society and the pleasure of the Creator and through the ways like Zakat (compulsory charity) sadakka (charity as per his will), Ihsan (virtuous deeds). It should be confirmed that his deeds are led by fear, love and knowledge about the Creator. Muamin should be grateful to Allah for all blessings. Muamin does so. The vital point of knowledge is the logical evaluation of the Ultimate Supreme power and as knowledge increases evaluation becomes more accurate and clear and when reason and wisdom are raised to its perfection from all factors, the enlightenment that soul enjoys is Iman or Consciousness of True knowledge. Leaving behind the old horizon, it goes on expanding. That beacon of light makes the Soul reach the perfect state. Everything from Him and to Him, being pure, I enter the Holy Allah. Perfecting the presence of the Creator is the purpose of Iman. Qur'an defines Allah so Allah; no God except He. He is eternal. He protects everything. Neither sleep nor drowsiness affects Him. Everything in Heaven and in the world is His. Who is he to recommend before Him without His permission? He knows their past and future. They cannot understand anything that He does not wish. His supremacy is spread all over the world and the sky. He is not wearied of protecting those. He is great and noble."(H.Q.2:255). "Allah is the Light of the heaven and the earth. The example of His light is like a niche within which is a lamp: the lamp is with in glass, the glass as if it were a sparkling star lit from [the oil of] a blessed olive tree, neither of the east nor of the west, whose oil would almost glow even if untouched by fire. Light upon light .Allah guides to His light whom He will. And Allah presents examples for the people, and Allah is knowing of all things"(H.Q.24:35).

Chapter 4
Theory of Monotheism

Devotion is the foundation stone of Islam. It is the initiative to knowledge and karma. It is to study how it is agreeable to other theories of religions.

The nature of God in Hinduism was a tradition of Indian thought which always discussed the aim of life, relation between Soul and Over Soul. Even in the first decades of Indian thought, the wrongs in the religious faith were corrected by reasoning. The progress of religion from Vedic hymns to Upanishads bears testimony to its growth. The most surprising deep insight in to the depth of mysteries of the universe is the un- surpassing trait of Indian thought, which indicates progress of the religion from Veda to Upanishads. Monotheism is the special feature of Rig veda. But the Monotheism of modern period became more clear and strong. When a concept of God arises, Monotheism becomes inevitable. With the growth of great insight in to the activities of Nature and God, many Gods are merged in to one. To believe in the laws of Nature means believe in Monotheism. As the result, blind beliefs became inactive. An inborn awareness about One God is originated. In the presence of this one reality the differences among Hindus, Christians, Aryan, Dravidian, Muslim, Jews and Heathen or Unbeliever faded out. All religions are shadows that ideology, though known in many names. In the text 'Indian Thought' Dr. Radha krishnan reveals "God is regarded as the Cosmic- guardian of all beings in Yajur veda and Adharva veda. It resembles to the references to Allah in the Holy Qur'an." It is said in Krishna Yajur veda "All salutations are to you who is the guardian of, marshy places, village tracks, lands, houses, valleys, trees, bushes, resting places, moonlight, plants, branches, leaves, caves, terrific forests, lakes, rivers, mist and dust (Chapter 4 Manthra 4-6). The epithets given to Allah in the Holy Qur'an are similar to it.

Lord of sky and earth Lord of great throne, Lord of stars and planets, Lord of the people, Lord of Sunrise and Sunset, My Lord, Your Lord, Their Lord, Lord of those, and Lord of all worlds. Adharva Veda says that God is Omniscient, he is very close to man He is aware of every movement of man. (Whether you walk, lay, getup, stand and laugh secretly Varuna will know it. When two people talk secretly, He is there as Third man. He knows their secret talk" (canton 4: Varga16 Mantra 8). This statement is similar to the descriptions of Allah in the Holy Qur'an. "Know you not the truth that Allah knows every thing in the Sky and the Earth? Allah is surely the Fourth Man when three people talk secretly. When five people talk secretly, Allah is there as the Sixth Man, whether the number lessens or increases He is there. Where ever they are He is with them. He has deep knowledge about everything" (H.Q.58:7). "Surely it is I that created Man. I know everything he feels. I am more close to him than his wind pipe" (H.Q.50:16).This One Truth is repeated in the pages of the text, 'Islamic Ideology.' "It is surprise that the instinctive awareness of One God was in the beginning": said Dr.Radhakrishnan. Islamic view is that this feeling took its origin along with the origin of man. Its origin is not logic; but revelation. Logic is a support to it. No time and place is there where a Prophet has not been sent. Qur'an teaches that it is undoubtedly clear that there was Prophet in India. The natural awareness of One God itself is the gift of God, says Islam.

Jewism was rooted in Monotheism. The holy text Thou rat (Thora) was given to Moose (Moses) the Prophet and spiritual preceptor of Jews. The Jews who fled from the native land due to the attack of Palestine by Assyrian king Nabukthu Nasser, lost everything including their Holy Text. Later one among them wrote a Thou rat from memory was subjected to many additions and deletions and in spirit it turned to be Polytheism. Monotheism of Jewish religion is revealed by Qur'an, 'Whom do you obey after me' when Yaakoov on his deathbed asked to his sons they said "We obey your God itself. The one God, Lord of your father, Ibrahim, Ismail and Is hack. We will live obeying them" (H.Q.2:133).

Jesus (Isa) the founder of Christianity was the last Prophet in the line of Bane- Israel, the descendant of Abraham. The text given to him is Inchil or New Commandments, The Bible). Though Qur'an does not agree with the idea of God's Son, Father, Son and Holy

Ghost and Crusification, both the religions have common tradition of line of Prophets. These two religions have resemblances as world religions having strict belief in moral principles, the ultimate aim of reaching God and faith in God.

Buddhism and Jainism deny the presence of an original cause, worship great men who are messengers of God and rooted in Ahimsa. Buddhist and Jain principles are not spiritual thoughts centered round God- these are intended to seek and find out God in man's soul by using inner eyes and also suggests means to attain (Nirvana) salvation. No need of God either for Creation or Destruction, says Jainism. The science of Morality is almost the same in both Buddhism and Jainism. The view of life seen in these religions is the sadness of life and the means for release is sacrifice, self-control and deep rooted morality. All the religions give primary importance to morality. But more preferable is to persuade for accepting morality than enforcing.

Chapter 5
Thou hid

Belief in the Oneness of Allah, protector of the Universe, is Thou hid or Monotheism. It is the central point of Islamic faith. It should be believed that He is not only the Supreme power that creates, protects and destroys the Universe, but He has all the special powers and rights of the divine power and none has any role in it. This stress on the Oneness of the Creator is the peculiarity of Islamic faith. The true ideal is that "Your God is one. He is love and mercy. No God except Him" is spread throughout Qur'an.

One ruler to one country, one manager in a factory and, one driver in a vehicle, this is the universal law. Two forces with equal powers are impracticable and dangerous. In such a situation there will be competition and struggle. Peace and serenity will not prevail in such a condition. But the order and system in the Universe reveals that there are no such two forces in the world because if it existed, the existence of the world would have been in danger. Holy Qur'an says "Allah has not created any child. No other God with him, if it had been so, each God would have exerted power and tried to subdue each other. But Allah is purer than what they describe" (H.Q.23:91).

The Oneness of the Creator has been accepted by all religions. It is the essence and gist of teachings of all Prophets. There was no difference of opinion regarding it among them.

Holy Qur'an says "Prophet you tell O believers! you come to a principle agreeable to you and we. Obey not anyone except Allah. Do not admit any one in Him Do not make any one as patrons except he" (H.Q.3:64).

Though ancient religions had Polytheistic beliefs and rituals basically they too accepted Mono theism. The Polytheists in Arabia, believed neither in Prophets nor in Divine religions, had accepted Allah, The One, as the Lord of the Universe. The natural call of human mind is also One God. Qur'an says that in moments of helplessness man prays to the One God. "Later when a misfortune affects you, you call and pray to Him" (H.Q.16:53).

Hundreds of evidences have been spread all through the universe to declare the existence and Oneness of the Creator. Man's wisdom and inner mind declares that it is truth. But the proud mind refuses to accept the truth. Qur'an says "Your God is One God. The minds of those who do not believe in life after death by pride refuses to accept the reality" (H.Q.16:22).

The basic slogan of Monotheism in Islam is "La Ilaha Illallahu" (No Ilaha except Allah)"Ilaha means he who is qualified to Ibadath. Ibadath means worship, obedience and submission. Monotheism in Islam means not that whether there is God or He is the One. On the contrary it should be believed that, He is the Cosmic Creator, Owner, Ruler and Controller. He supplies all the resources required for the survival of all beings in the Universe Only. He supplies energy for their existence. He alone has claim over all the aspects of Sovereignty. None has any role or part in it. He has all aspects of Divinity. He sees everything on the Earth and in the Sky. He has direct and subtle knowledge about everything. His knowledge is not confined to the present Time alone. He contains in Himself Past and Future. He alone has invisible knowledge and insight to look in to everything. He has no beginning. He is eternal. All others except Him are moral. He is reasonable and He lives self. His deeds are logical and motivated. He is invincible and omnipotent. He gives reward to all deeds, good for goodness and evil for evil deeds. In spite of all, He is one. These qualities are His.

These are the wishes of those who believe in Allah and His Oneness. All creations on the Earth and the Sky are of Allah. Everything is under his control and dependence. His creations have no ability or power of their own except those given by the generosity and blessings of great Allah. Those abilities may exist or die according to the will of Allah. You should not accept anything as guardian or Lord of the Universe except Allah.

Accept Him only as one who can solve all the difficulties and can fulfill the needs of man. He alone can help and protect and know the secrets. All the things of man are bound to His decisions and are in his jurisdiction. None can do good or harm help or punish except He. So not to be afraid of anyone else; should not entrust any one display no devotion to anyone except He.

We should not worship anyone except Allah. Bow head only before Him. Prostrate only to Him. Unconditional obedience and love should be dedicated only to He, should not pray to anyone except Him. He alone has claim over all kinds of worshipping. Ask for help from invisible centers only to Him. We should not even imagine of any one who can exert influence in the Judgment of God or divine deeds. Seek no help from others. Accept no mediators to Allah. Pray only to Him.

Purity of life and social goodness based on individual culture are the values upheld by Islamic values. Its result is connected with the other world. A system of rule based God's rules is only a material product. If we can live obeying God's guidelines and worship and keep up accuracy, nothing will lose to the sovereignty of Allah or any defect to Thou hid. Not the system, but the attitude is to be changed.

Chapter 6
Shirk or Polytheism

Shirk means to make a participant. To give participation to a thing in the qualities and gist of Allah is called as Shirk in Islamic language. All that is analogical to thou hid is called Shirk. Divine religions or Prophets have not taught to believe in Polytheism. Even the religions that believe in multi religions admit that their real God is one. The mind of a Polytheist is always in struggle. Whom should he dedicate? Whom does he pray? He always perturbed by the question. Holy Qur'an depicts the mental state of a Polytheist in a simile: "One man, many people are under him. They always quarrel. Another man he lives under one master. Are these people alike"? (H.Q.39:29).

The hollowness of Polytheism is revealed thus. "If anyone has employed a sharer to Allah he is like one fell from the sky. Birds will carry him. Or he will be carried away to a distant place."(H.Q.22:31) "O men! Here is a simile you carefully listen to it. The things you pray deserting Allah, do not create a fly. Even if they are united, they cannot get anything in return (Help), if the fly has taken anything by force. The prayer and the one prayed for are equally weak" (H.Q.22:73). "The simile of those who make others patrons except Allah is like a spider. It made a house. The weakest of the houses is that of a spider (Alas!) if they had been sensible!"(H. K.29:41).

Holy Qur'an describes the Shirk as serious crime and unpardonable sin because it gives the status of the Creator and powers and rights to some one else "Allah does not forgive that He is shared. All other things He will forgive. Those who think of sharers with Allah do great crime "(H.Q.4:8). "————Sure, Shirk is a great crime" (H.Q.31:13).

Accept the greatness and sovereignty of Allah. At the same time turns away from Him and move with the disobedient fellows and do their practices- This is Shirk itself. Thou hid is to surrender the whole of life to the Cosmic Lord. It is a faithful Shirk if anyone else is accepted with Allah for prayer, worshipping and implicit obedience.

And we request for help only to Him. So when we worship others who are not Cosmic Lords that is equal to make sharers to Allah. When we practice self made laws and not of Allah's, even if it is truth and justice, it is like making them equal to God. Both these are Shirk. —Whether call them God or not those in whose name offerings are made and accept unconditionally the laws made, they too become sharers of the Creator.

Chapter 7
Islamic Faith

1) Malakkukal [Angels]

The second factor of true faith in Iman is faith in Malakukal or Angels, the invisible creations who act according to the commands of Allah. We cannot imagine the form or appearance of these who live in another world, except the descriptions given in Qur'an. There is similar faith in other religions too. It is to imagine that the Angels of Christianity and gods and goddesses of Hinduism are these.' Amsaspath what the Parses believe is like that. All these people give forms and worship these wonderful phenomena. But Qur'an explains that this understanding is wrong. Man is the greatest of creations and Angels has only bowed before man. Man does not see The Creator directly .The messages from the Creator reaches to man through Angels. "Allah choses messengers from Angels and man."(H.Q.22:75).They have noble character unlike man. They do no wrongs. They have no feeling of the self. They do not disobey the commands of Allah. "All the Angels in the sky and the earth live abiding by Allah and prostrate to Him. They display no pride. They fear the Lord who is above them. They do what is ordered to them." (H.Q.16:49—50)They act as helpers in the ruling of the universe. Qur'an says that Angels appreciates man and prays for him to Allah. They will pray for the redemption of man from sin. They will curse the evil doers and they will be treated brutally in the other world, Qur'an reminds man. In short, Angels are those who always obey Allah and his orders. They go on singing hymns and prayers of God. Faith in the invisible powers is declared as a part of Iman.

2) Holy Texts

The Holy Texts are the divine messages that give guidance to man from the very origin of humanity. In the beginning man lived as one community. Later when he grew up intellectually and comforts developed changes happened in behavior and character. So man controlled the ways of life and he made an order and discipline in life style according to the time and place. New guidelines and laws became necessary. In order to give warning to the man who went astray from God and give guidance Allah was used to send Prophets from time to time. "Man was only a single community. Later they separated into different categories. Then He sent Prophets to give warning and happy news to man. To declare judgment in the things where man was divided, Allah sent Holy Text along with Truth. But those who were given Texts stood divided –" (H.Q.2:213).All these Holy Texts were fixed on only one basic principle. That is there is no Creator except Allah and obedience and surrender are only before Him. Religion based on this principle is called 'Dee nil Islam' (Islamic Religion) and those who live abiding by it are known as Muslims. The religion originated on the earth is thus Islam itself. All religions declare that "Allah has given to you the name Muslims in the Qur'an and Vedas before it."(H.Q.22:78).

So it is understood that in the beginning of human race human community was only one and their religion Islam. According to time, place, situations and needs, new Holy Texts and Prophets appeared having new instructions. There is no change in basic principle. All the Holy Texts were like links in a chain, approving each other. Holy Texts comes to an end with the Holy Qur'an.

Qur'an does not state in detail to which people and periods Holy Texts were given. No community has passed by without a Prophet. No need of saying that exhortation has taken place from time to time. Still in Qur'an there is a "list of 25 Prophets and Vedas and Texts were supplied to them" (H.Q.6:84-86). But not so all the Holy texts contain the commands given by Allah to humanity from time to time and in a particular point in the development of culture, with the origin of Qur'an, the Holy Text given to Mohammad (S.A.) the series of Veda is completed. It is notes mentioned which Texts have been given among these 25 Prophets. Holy Qur'an refers mainly about Thaurath (Thora) given to Musa (A) or Moses, Sab oar given to Davood (A) or David, Inchil (The Bible)given to Isa (A) or Jesus and the fourth and last is Fur khan or Qur'an given to Mohammed (S.A). This faith is the part of Iman. Holy Qur'an exists still in all its purity without any changes. A special chapter is allotted to Holy Qur'an.

3) Prophets

To have faith in the Prophets is a part of Iman. Allah has sent countless Prophets in the world to guide humanity in the proper way. As stated that no age passed by without Prophets, we can understand that numerous Prophets are born in the world.

All the Prophets sent in to the world are human beings alone. It is necessary for exhortation. "No messenger has been sent by me that was not in the language of the people" (14:4) declares Qur'an. None can acquire the status of Prophet-hood by self- effort. Allah selects some one as Prophets. They were embodiments of all virtuous qualities. They were having all emotional states like hunger, thirstiness, passion and death.

The duty of Prophets is to reach the message getting through Jib reel [Gab real] from Allah to the people. All these missions are meant to establish the Oneness and sovereignty of Allah and it contains principles and guidelines to lead the people in the right way. Prophets are expected to reform the society .They optimistically educate people hoping that people will obey them one day or another day. Their aim is not destruction but renovation.

It is ordered in the Qur'an to accept all Prophets without denying the former Prophets. "No difference is attributed among the messengers of Allah" (H.Q.2:285).It is told so to the followers. So whenever the name of a Prophet is mentioned, Muslims pray for all blessings of Allah over them. The faith of a Muslim not to accept the former Prophets and believe only in Mohammad (S) is not right. Allah clearly states. "O! You believed believe in Allah and His messenger, the Holy Book that He sent down upon His messenger and the Scripture which He sent down before. And whoever disbelieves in Allah His angels His book His messengers and the Last Day have certainly gone astray."(H.Q.4:136).

Mohammed is the only Prophet who has been subjected to historical intensive study among the world leaders. No man is more reputed than He. He is very close to human race. No man is as merciful as He. The study of Qur'an takes man to a safer and nobler position in spiritual ways. It discourages Sanyasm and Mats which do harm to humanity. However since each religion functions based on the root of Holy Text, it helps for a comparative study.

4) Last Day

Faith in the end of the world and Day of Judgment is apart of Iman. There is an end to the Universe and the life. Universal end none knows when it happen. "It will happen soon" says Qur'an "a day which indicates a terrible end." Qur'an explains "a single clarion and when by lifting up the earth and mountains, hit the great event will take place. The Sky will break and it will become weak. On the day He will do everything by himself. Supremacy is for Allah on the day of blowing the clarion" (H.Q.6:73).

On the terrible day of blowing clarion, all men will run in fright. None thinks of anyone else. By fear his eyes will become pale and life less. The tongue will withdraw to inside. What happened to the earth? Where should we go? He asked himself. Allah says "O men! Beware of your Protector (About to come). The reverberation of that moment is a great event. The day when you see it, the women who feed their breast will forget the feeding children. All the pregnant women will give birth to children. You can see that man is affected by intoxication. Really he is not affected by intoxication, but Allah's punishment will be very terrific" (H.Q.22:1-2). When the Sun is covered, stars slipped down, mountains removed, the full-term she- camels neglected, wild animals come in group, the oceans are filled with flame" (H.Q.81:1-6). "eyes silenced by fear, Moon's light faded out and the Sun and the Moon come together, man will ask where to escape?"(H.Q.75:7-10) "When the sky breaks, stars scatter into pieces and the sea and the rivers flow away"(H.Q.82:1-3). "When the earth is made tremble, the earth pushes its weight to outside, man ask what happened to it, earth will get the news that the Lord has instructed." (H.Q.99:1-15). "A terrific tragedy: what is the terrific tragedy? You know what it is? The day man is scattered like butterflies."(H.Q.101:1-5). "When the graves are opened the deeds man has done and not done will become clear" (H.Q.8:24-5). "To see the results of man's deeds, they will come from graves as scattered. If anyone has done an atom of goodness; He will see that. If done an atom of evil He will see that too" (H.Q.99:6-8).

"Then whose balance weighs down, he is in a satisfied state; whose balance is weightless, his abode will be 'Havia'. You know what is this 'Havia?' It is fire with terrible heat."(H.Q.101:6-11). "That deluge will take place soon."(H.Q.7:187). "When the event that is going to happen is over nothing will exist to deny its possibility."(H.Q.56:1-12).What the Qur'an words reveal is that each and everything and even to the universe has a Last day.

5) Life in the other world

Soul or Nafs is responsible for all mental and physical activities. All human souls have to answer for their deeds in this world to Allah. He will give reward to each deed. Death is not an end; only a turning point. When soul travels from a physical atmosphere to a spiritual one, it loses its physical form. That is death or leaving of body. As Soul does not die, it reaches the presence of Allah in an invisible world. Human life is described as having three states.

1) Birth through the media of body and ends with death, worldly life.

2) The state after death. The soul enjoys the pleasures and sorrows or life in 'Bersakh.'

3) Eternal life, life between the soul at Bersakh and the body resurrected after death.

The three sources of man's stage- physical, righteous and spiritual are called as Nafs ammara Nafs Lavvama and Nafs muthma Inna. Nafs ammara is the soul that moves to evils and wrongs. That is the animal state of the body. The soul that scolds itself for its crimes is called Nafs lavvama. The soul that attained eternal peace by God's grace is called Nafs Muthma Inna. Words in the Qur'an is thus "Vala ukkesimu binnafsi- lavvama": "I swear in the name of the soul that repents for its wrong deeds and scolds itself" Return as attained eternal peace by God's grace and you satisfied in Him and He satisfied in you" (H.Q.89:27-28). These three states are appear as two stages in our view, the stage of life from birth to death. Next, Life in Bersakh since death and eternal life since resurrection and it includes life after death.

Faith in the end of this world and Day of Judgment is a part of Iman. "The evil deeds of all people are tied up with them. On the day of Resurrection I will give a Text to him. He will see that it is opened. You read the Text you yourself is enough to present crimes against you" (H.Q.17:13-14). Allah tells about the Day of Judgment "None will punish as Allah does on that day."[To the righteous it will be said] "O reassured return your Lord well-pleased and pleasing [to Him] and enter among my [righteous] servants and enter my Paradise."(H.Q.89:25-29, 30).

Allah states about life in the other world "They are telling there is no life except this worldly life, we should never be resurrected" (H.Q.45:24). Allah says "Creation of you and resurrection are like doing it on a single person. No doubt Allah can see and hear everything." (H.Q.31:28). If they saw how they stood in the presence of the Guardian! Then he would ask "is it not truth?" They would say: "Yes, Our Guardian is the only Truth!" He (to them) would say. "Then you suffer the punishment for denying Truth." Those who denied that we should meet Allah would be damned. When the time comes they would lament. Alas! What a foolery we showed. "Then they would be carrying the burden of their sin on their back. How dirty is the weight they bear." (H.Q.6: 29, 30, 31).

The only Text, that describes neatly about the 'Last day' and life in the other world, is Qur'an itself.

Chapter 8
Islamic duties

"The religion that commands to live being subjected to Allah and His commands, to practice Namaskar in order and to give Zakat (Compulsory charity)and the correct religion is this itself"(H.Q.98:5). The foundation of Islamic religion is a noble system consisting of Six principles and Five duties. It is known as the five pillars of Islam: 1) Kalima 2) Namaskar. 3) Zakat. 4) Practicing Vows. 5) Hajj (Pilgrimage to Kaaba).

1) Kalima (Swearing)

It means that there is no God except Allah and Mohammed is His Prophet. Allah is One, no partner to Him. Mohammed is His slave and true messenger. Believe it and glorify His greatness and purity. Birth death evil and goodness are his deeds. Recognition and declaration of these are 'Kalimathushahadathu.' Real Islamic believer is he who recognizes Allah, His, greatness and Oneness, sovereignty and dedicates every thing to Him and live according to it. He should have faith in the Prophet Mohammad as the messenger and Prophet of God. 'No God except Allah' is the important aspect of Iman. From the beginning of man Prophets have been sent to lead to Monotheism. But man turned to Polytheism. Instead of probing into the wonders of Nature and its mysteries and enjoying it, illiterate people worshipped Gods in the grass, stones and flies. Allah has repeatedly told the people to accept Mohammed only as the messenger of Allah. To keep up the purity of Oneness (Thou hid) the second part of Kalima is said as 'Mohammad is the messenger of Allah'. (Mohammad S.A) Tell: "O, men I am a messenger coming from Allah who is the Lord of the Sky and the Earth, no God except He" (H.Q.7:158).

The greatness of Kalima is recorded thus. Abudargh (Ra) says. His Excellence spoke "anyone who has been a witness to the truth that there is none except Allah to be worshipped and died thus will certainly enter Heaven, even if he has stolen and seduced".

2) Namaskar

Every religion has its own system of worshipping. All of them worship Gods or their deities in different manners. No priesthood in Islam. All good deeds and prayers of Muslim are included in worshipping. Namaskar is noblest form of prayer. Every sensible adult should practice it. It is compulsory ritual to a Muslim. Some concessions have been granted in certain contexts. Menstruated and delivered women should not do it until they are purified. They should clean their body by bathing. Namaskar is done five times a day in different timings. It is an act to be done with discipline and balance of mind. That means the body as well as the place should be pure. The whole body should be covered. Apart from the cleanliness of body, parts – cleaning (Vulu) should be done. Vulu means wash mouth and nostrils with clean water. Wash face elaborately. Wash hands along with knee, wash palm and massage the inner and outer parts of head and ears, wash legs along with. Repeat it three times. To sit with right side projected is noble and sit in order as time demands. It is necessary. In a stage of illness when water cannot be touched or because of the scarcity of it, 'Thayyamum' is carried out. Thayyamum means both two palms touch on clean earth or dry clean surface, massage gently face with palms and the part up to the fingers of hand. So start Namaskar facing the Mosque in Mecca by strictly following discipline.

All the Muslims in the world do Namaskar facing towards one center (Kaaba). It is the first house built for worshipping the Creator. By doing so a universal unity is maintained and also is meant that all the Muslims believe in the' same culture and brotherhood'.

Namaskar is done in certain stages. The sitting poses completed in one circle in some stages are called 'Rekkaouth.' Do 'Niyyathu' with equanimity of mind standing erect facing Kaaba. It should be imagined in mind. Imagine this Namaskar, this much Rekkaouth, I prostrate to the Allah's facing quibla.The name of the Namaskar is the reminder of the time of Namaskar. Subahi, Lugar, Assar, Maghreb, Isha are the

names of Namaskar. Two Rekkaouth to Subahi three rekkaouth to
Maarib and four to the others for doing Namaskar. Five times Namaskar
is 'Furze' (Compulsory). The other Namaskar are known as Sunnathu.
A Muslim should definitely do 'Furze' and if not done, it is punishable.
If 'Sunnathu' is done it is rewarded and no punishment if not done.
Lifting two hands equal to the shoulder along with Niyyathu pronounce
'Allah Akbar' (Allah, the greatest) and join two hands on the breast
stand by placing right hand over the left hand. This pose is called
'Thakbirathul Ihram'- dedicate yourself to Allah. And after swearing
the oath, read the first chapter 'Fathiha' of Qur'an and chant some
words or one chapter from Qur'an. Second pose, 'Ruckus 'from the
first pose by uttering 'Allah Akbar' place two hands on two knees and
bow head. This is called Rekkaouth. Say three times in this state
'Subbuhanarabbiyal alim'(Glory to my great Lord). Third pose ;Stand
erect from 'Ruckus, say 'Rabbana lakkal hamdu' (Our Lord!, all glories
are to you).Fourth pose; Utter 'Allah Akbar' from third pose do
'Sujud'(Prostrate). It is a pose when fingers of feet, knees, front arms
and forehead touch the ground. Utter three times in that pose
'Subbuhanarabbiyal Aaala' (Glory to my great Lord)- this is the first
Sujud. Fifth pose; rise from Sujud, say 'Allah Akbar' stick the tip of
right feet and turn left feet to right and sit on it in a peculiar style. At this
time 'Allahumma rubbigfirli' (Allah, forgive me —), begins the prayer.
Sixth pose-again chant Thakbir once again and do 'sujud '(Prostrate)
(Second Sujud).Now one 'Rekkaouth' is completed. After second 'Sujud'
in the First 'Rekkaouth' utter 'Allah Akbar' and rise prostrate one more
'Rekkaouth'. That is repetition of what is done in the first 'Rekkaouth.'
After doing the second 'Sujud' rise and sit as mentioned above. In this
pose chant the prayer 'Athahiyyath.' On occasions when more than two
'Rekkaouth' are to be prostrated, rise again and complete the rest of
'Rekkaouth.' After completing all the 'Rekkaouth', chant 'Dua' (Prayer)
and the prayer with the meaning given below: As you blessed, Allah,
Ibrahim and his followers, bless Mohammad and his followers, as you
did favor to Ibrahim and his followers, do favor to Mohammad and
his followers sure you are great and glorified. After this chant the
prayer to escape from sins, utter 'Assalamu Alaikum', turn face to right
and repeating the prayer turn face to the left and ends the Namaskar.

Timings of Namaskar

1) Fajr (Subahi—Dawn) namaskar in between sunrise and morning. It is done in two 'Rekkaouth'

2) Luhar (midday) namaskar when the sun moves from its summit: Four rekkaouth.

3) Assar namaskar (evening) when the sun reaches to set: four rekkaouth.

4) MagaribNamaskar (namaskar at dusk) soon after sunset: three rekkaouth

5) Isha namaskar (night namaskar) from sunset to midnight: four rekkaouth.

When it is time for namaskar a peculiar kind of horn comes from the Mosques for doing namaskar and getting success in life. This is known as 'Banku or Athan'- 'Allah is the greatest one', four times. Non to be worshipped except Allah, two times; come soon for Namaskar, two times; come in hurry for success –two times. Allah is great -two times. No God except Allah, once—'Banku' is a loud call in Arabic words with the above said meaning.

It is a noble thing to pray in group under the leadership of a leader (Imam).It is more a virtuous thing when it is in the Mosque. No caste or religious discriminations are there. The rich, the poor, the ruler and the ruled, the black and the white, jostle together in group prayer Women stand in a particular place or at the back row. One day in a week—Friday—a special group prayer is conducted on the day. This group prayer conducted instead of Midday prayer is known as 'Juma.' This Namaskar is two rekkaouth. Before the Namaskar the leader (Imam) gives moral advice for success in this world and the other world. This gospel is called as 'Khuthuba.' In spite of the five namaskars there are 'Sunnath' namaskars in two rekkaouth. The Namaskar conducted during ram san nights, called 'Tharaveeh' and those before and after the compulsory Namaskar and those performed for multi purposes like getting rain and at the time of eclipse are all in this category. There is separate Namaskar for the dead (Mayyath Namaskar). In this there is neither bowing nor bending head. Namaskar influences man spiritually and mentally. Kaaba is the first worshipping centre built in the world to worship the Lord of the Universe with fear and devotion, standing in a neat and tidy place and dressed in neat and fresh dress as one free from all impurities and contains the gist of Prophet's statement that though we do not see Him, He sees us. We should dedicate all our wishes and hopes to the only one Creator and attribute no place to mediators and pray with purity of heart. This is the undercurrent and gist of prayer. It is an interview and a dialogue of man with his Creator. It is heart communication for the spiritual elevation of man. It helps to attain release from sin and mental purity. "I here by being obedient and straight forward turn my face to the Creator who created the sky and the earth. I am not one to admit any one in the powers and authority of Allah. My Namaskar, life, death and prayers are only due to the protector of the Universe. He has no share. I am told to live so. I am in the group of obedient people." So swearing in the presence of Allah, man directly prays to Him. These prayers are Namaskar. It is believed that it should be in Arabic language. However Namaskar should be done with proper knowledge. "Those who do Namaskar as a pretense and not doing even a simple help to others have more danger" (H.Q.107:4-7). Do Namaskar understanding the gravity of words in the Qur'an. "The reward for those who give zakat believe in the Truth and do virtuous deeds, is in the Protector. They have nothing to fear. No reason for them to be worried"(H.Q.2:227). This firm faith is the essence of prayer. It is inevitable to a Muslim. Some concessions have been allowed in state of illness, war and travelling. If not able to prostrate, do it by sitting, lying, gestures, or in mind. Namaskar at the time of travel and war can be done in brief. It can be done even in Vehicles. If difficult to face 'quibla', avoid it. But punctuality is a prominent factor

Namaskar is the most important thing in Islamic life. Those who do not do Namaskar have not been treated as Muslims. It was a sign to distinguish between Muslims and non- Muslims. Qur'an warns that if evil deeds and forbidden acts are not avoided when Namaskar is done, it may cause the death of values of life and after death such a man will enter hellish fire as despised and neglected. Namaskar gives joy and happiness in moments of frustration and sadness. It gives hope and relief to him. It gives courage and strength to face any problems in life. Muslims who do Namaskar with fear and devotion would get victory in this life and the other life. The understanding, that God's blessings can be achieved by occasional prayer or Pooja after leading a life of selfish interests and exploitation by yielding to wishes and passions and become sinful, has no value in Islam. Islam considers Namaskar a part of routine life. Five times' Namaskar on a day have been insisted to each Muslim. Each Namaskar strengthens the base of his life. 'Just like a man who daily baths five times in a river is not affected by dirtiness those who does five time's Namaskar on a day will be sinless': Prophet stated.

Compulsory Charity (Zakat)

The system of Sakkath and its details remain as a revolutionary challenge against the economic system in the world. Charity to poor people is not a novel thing. But zakat is not a charity. There are other virtuous deeds in Islam except 'zakat-that is not 'Zakat' but 'Sadakka.' Zakat is one among the five pillars of Islamic mansion. The word Zakat means, growth, purity and contentment. Its technical meaning is to give a noble part of one's wealth in order to purify his wealth. In priority zakat is next to Namaskar in Islam. It has been often referred to in Qur'an as an important act. Zakat is public property collected compulsorily from wealthy Muslims in a fixed proportion of Rs2.5%. It is a means to purify property from contamination and refine it. It will purify the mind of the owner and his wealth would increase. "You collect zakat from them. By that purify and refine them—"(H.Q.9:103). Allah orders to Mohammad (Sa) zakat is compulsory to, gold above 85gm (2.5%), Silver (2.5%), Solid things (20%), Commodities for sale (2.5%) products (10%), cattle etc. zakat to be given to money deposits (2%), Bonds (3%), Shares (4%), cattle: camels up to four no's : no zakat, camels from 5 to 9:1 camel, from 10 to14 : 2, from 15 to 19 :3 camels, upto 29 cows have no zakat. From 30 to 39: 2 calves aged 1 year from 40 to 59: 1 calf aged 2 years, and 39 lambs have no Zakat. From 40 to 120: 1 lamb from 121 to 200: 2 lambs, from 201 to 300:3 lambs." Zakat is a claim only to poor dependents, helpless ones, those working for zakat (collection and distribution) those to be tamed (new believers) method to release from slavery, those who live as debtors, and, believers in God. Allah is a profound scholar and a skilled diplomat."(H.Q.9:60). The life of a Muslim is based on the system 'Thou heed' (Monotheism). The ownership of the universe is not to any individuals, or society; only to Allah. He has given the right for consumption of wealth to man." He has created everything in the world for you — (H. K.2:29). Production of food is the right of man. But food is the monopoly of any one. Ownership of all wealth and the right of consumption are to

Allah and man respectively. On the basis of Allah's words none can claim right over Desert, Wild animals, Sea Resources, Minerals. These are to be considered as public property. Approving these general rules, certain rights have been given to individuals. Work, sacrifice and service of the individual are its basis. Special rights have been rendered to individuals on the hunted animal barren land made fertile, and income from the transaction of agricultural products. Public property belongs to Allah and his Prophet. The Prophet has right to give barren land to any one. After the Prophet, Islamic government has right to give the property to someone. If one has to make a claim over the land he should make it an agricultural land. If the land is kept barren for three years, it should be confiscated from him. Then confiscate the surplus land of the claim and share it among the landless people. That is the Islamic rule. In brief public property and its uses are subjected to rules and laws. Government has right to collect zakat, if necessary force can be used. From the point of economics, zakat is the first implemented orderly and systematic tax in the world. When Islamic rule existed zakat was collected in a regular proportion and remitted in the public treasuries. Separate department and officers were there. It was strict that the officers should be honest and just. Before the advent of Islamic rule it was irregular, selfish and a kind of exploitation of the poor.

After giving financial help to those who deserve, the rest of the fund is used for constructing Hospitals, Orphanages, Inns, and Factories and supplying tools to workers and give help to poor students and encourage righteous deeds. These are the duties of the government

Another compulsory charity is 'Fithirzakat.' It is a charity given on the Perennial day of ramzan to eat food lavishly for all people. The Muslim Community as a whole to celebrate the day of Id. There should be none with out food for eating. It is also a remedy for any relapse which may happen in the days of vows. Each Muslim would give one 'saau' (2.220gm) food to all his dependants. It is better to collect and distribute it among the people. Voluntary charity to poor people is not zakat. That is called 'Sadakka.' Islam encourages the act of giving 'Sadakka.' The virtuous deeds in the limit of 'Sadakka' are protecting parents, relatives and the helpless. Feeding the animals and birds also is 'Sadakka.' Donation to organizations societies and giving tools to workers and helping them, are 'Sadakka.' Good behavior, pleasant talk warm welcome are regarded as 'Sadakka.'

4) Practice of Vow (Fasting)

From time immemorial some kind of practice of Vow existed among all sects of people in the world. In ancient Egypt people irrespective of age has practiced Vow in connection with their festivals. The priests among them too had practiced it from seven days to one and a half month in a year. It had existed in China too. They were used to take Vow in days of misfortune and misery without swallowing even saliva. Vow of silence was very popular in Greece. It was their habit to sit cross legged devotedly for some fixed days before starting something. Women were more strict it doing vow than men. Silence of Vow and Celibacy were part of Hind life in India. Even now it is being practiced by devotees. There had been many Sanyasins in India who gave up water and food and chose forest life for the purification of soul. Vows had been attributed to Jews. It is said their Prophet Moses (A.S.) had practiced 40 days Vow. It is their habit to practice Vow in group when disasters take place. They were commanded to practice Vow regret to crimes and wrongs.

Their Holy Text Thaurath (Thora) instructs to practice Vow in certain days in a year. According to the Holy Text of Jews (Thora, Old Testament) the Christians who came later also had practiced Vow. Ramzan is the month in which the Holy Qur'an is presented as a guideline with clear evidences of truth and moral principles. "Let all present in your group in that (in that month) practice Vow" (H.Q.2:185). "True believers, you are hereby strictly ordered to practice Vow as told to your predecessors. It is to keep up accuracy" (H.Q.2:183). It was told in the former Texts to keep up Vows. Vow is meant to keep away man from sin. Compulsory Vow is done in a particular month. It was in that month The Holy Qur'an which can differentiate between truth and falsehood. When the crescent moon appears in the western horizon Vow begins from the next morning. With the sunset of the day one Vow is completed. This practice is continued till the beginning of shavval month. The aim of Vow is not giving up food and pleasures of life, but self -control and do no sin either by mind, words or deeds. Vow is a shield. If anyone practices Vow, he should not speak evil words. 'If anyone scolds him or quarrels with him, let them say I am a Vower' (Bukhari Muslim). A Vower gets spiritual courage and patience to endure difficulties in life. Allah says "a Vower gives up food and water for me.

I will reward him". Hoping for the blessings of Allah, a Muslim practices Vow. It is a secret understanding between Allah and his slave. One who does it accurately and strictly will get many blessings from Allah. He gets worldly benefits too. It helps to regularize the imbalance of the body and purifies the stomach and gives rest to digestive system. You practice Vow you will get hygienic benefits. "Practice of Vow is only for limited days" says the prophet. But if anyone becomes sick or in journey (The number left out) should be completed in other days. Those who are unable to practice Vow (if gives up Vow) should give food to a poor man as repentance. If anyone does good voluntarily it is for him. "If you have consciousness, it is better to practice Vow" (H.Q.2:184). Contact with your wife is permitted on the nights of Vow. They are clothes to you and you are clothes to them. Being obliged to your body you are doing unjust things, Allah knows. You are forgiven by Him. So till you can identify the white thread from the black thread (Until morning) you live with them. You wish, eat and drink what Allah has decided for you. After that (From morning) until night begins to continue Vow" (H.Q.2:187). "Allah proposes to give you comfort and not to put in difficulty. All these are to make you complete the number and to glorify his greatness and show gratitude for giving guidelines" (H.Q.2:185). The Muslims of early period lived separated from their wives. It is only a torture and should not be repeated, your wrongs have been forgiven. Convenience has been arranged for doing Namaskar with out any difficulty. The above said maxims are to exhort people. No compromise in the practice of Vows in the month of Ramzan. Pregnant women and breast feeding women sick people and travelers are given concessions on the day and they should complete Vow on some other days. Women in menstruation should not do Vow. They would do it after some days. The food to begin Vow should be changed to early morning and the break of Vow should be soon after the Sunset.

Qur'an says the selection of Ramzan for Vow is very important. The origin of Qur'an was in that month. The night Qur'an is presented is called as 'Lailathulkhadhar'. Though cannot strictly say which the night is; it is in between the days of the month. The Vows in this month are more virtuous than the Vows in other months. It is ordered that the Qur'an should be read completely and did meditation. The Namaskar in Ramzan month is given more importance by the Prophet. As Ramzan month is a month when more rewards are given for virtuous deeds,

Muslims attach more significance to charity. In the old days Holy Texts tell about Vows. Later they curtailed some principles according to their will. It became a mere ritual. Experienced people say that self- control controls hunger, thirst and the soul. It is regarded as training for the progress of the soul. There are some other Vows practiced in other contexts. It is called 'Sunnathu Vow.' The important Vows among Sunnathu Vows are, Vows on the first six days except 'Id' .The Dulhaj Vow practiced by Muslims who do not go to Haj, 'The Vow of the Tenth day in the month of Muharram is to remind the death of Pharos by drowning and the rescue of Moses. Vows are to be practiced as repentance for wrong doings.'

5) Hajj

It means visit. It is the fifth compulsory item in Islam. It is holy visit to Kaaba. Visit to places is regarded as a means to make life contented and cheerful. World Muslims meet every year in Mecca. Historians say that the origin of all Semitic communities is from Arabs in Arabia. The most influential religions in the world, like Jewism. Christianity and Islam are originated from Semitic community. Holy Qur'an qualifies Arabia as'UmmulKhura' means the mother of villages. The Mecca city is a center of culture and civilization. ' Kaaba' in the holy Mecca is the first worshipping center in the world for worshipping the Creator of the world. It is not mentioned in the Holy Qur'an when it is built. The history of 'Kaaba' begins from the time of Abraham. It was damaged in the deluge before the Prophet-hood of Mohammed (Sa). It is reconstructed during the time of the Prophet. Qur'an explains this in detail. "Remember the occasion when Ibrahim and Ismail constructed it" (2:12). The first building as a blessing and a guide line to humanity was in Mecca. The worshipping place of the Prophet is included in it. (H.Q.3:96-97). Allah ordered Abraham to proclaim 'Kaaba' as the pilgrim center of humanity. "Proclaim to man about Hajj; so he would come on by foot and on riding on very lean camels" (H.Q.22:27).

As far as Muslims are concerned it is not only a pilgrim center but the origin of culture and human civilization. Muslims should do Namaskar by turning to the building in Mecca "You turn your face towards the prayer house"(2:144). There is a great message in this uniformity. There is no chance of becoming rivals among Muslims as they stand face to face at least five times a day. Hajj is not a practice started at the time of the last

Prophet Mohammed. History records that people had gone to Mecca for doing Hajj and cirrcumlocute Kaaba. Since three thousand years it has been in vogue. Allah told Ibrahim to keep Kaaba neat and tidy for those who come there for Namaskar and prayer. "If anyone enters in it they should do Hajj without fear and they are safe. It is their right. If any one denies it Allah is free from need of the worlds."(H.Q.3:97). All the healthy and rich Muslims should do Hajj.

Sahihul Bukhhari speaks about the role of women, Ayesha (Ra) asked we, women look upon Jihad the most sacred deed. Won't we fight? His majesty spoke : "No as far as you are concerned, noble duty is to perfect the holy Hajj."

Important deeds in Hajj

1) Ihram. 2) be present at Arafa. 3) Kaaba circumlocution. 4) Run seven times between Safa-marva hills 5) Shaving hair. If possible animal sacrifice to be done either alone or seven people together. If any of these is left out Hajj will not become perfect. Even though sacrifice is 'Sunnath' if any important item in Hajj is left, sacrifice becomes compulsory. Sacrifice is to be done after entering 'Ihram' and if any forbidden act is done.

Philosophical aspect of Hajj

Hajj has a philosophical aspect. Human life has become a mechanical phenomenon for the man who lost aims in day today life. His aim is to live however and so the soul in him is dead. Experience of Hajj changes lifeless situation. It is the reverse side of aimlessness; a protest against the control of evil powers. It enables man to escape from the network of mysteries of life. The horizon of man is widened and the path to eternity and the Omnipotent Allah are cleared by it.

Man's life is meaningless if no aim to get the nearness of Allah. We should join in all attempts to do Hajj and keep away from all desires that take away from Allah. Fulfill all liabilities before going for Hajj. Renunciation from anger and love towards relatives and foes should disappear. Write down a Will. All these steps are the procedures to death. Purity of the mind and our finance are affirmed by these deeds. This is the sign of farewell and the future of man. Thus we reach life as the part of eternity.

It represents man's return to Allah. He is one, limitless and unequalled. Return to Him is returning to goodness, perfection, beauty, power, knowledge and truth and reality. It is the path to eternity. On the way He gives us guidance.

It is in the month of 'Dulhaj.' Mecca is quiet and peaceful. There is protection and peace instead of hatred and fear. Proper atmosphere exists there for prayer. The commandment given to 'Ibrahim' reveals: "Proclaim to man about Hajj." "They will come to you walking and on tired animals"(H.Q 22:27).

Umra

It is a sacred act just like Hajj. But it can be done at any time. Some differences are there compared to Hajj. After finishing Kaaba circumlocution and seven times running among Safa-marva hills, remove hair and retire from Umra. It is better to do it before Hajj. Pilgrims who come from distant countries do Umra along with Hajj. Until the beginning of Thwavaf (Kaaba circumlocution) continue 'Thalbiyath.' After circumlocution should not chant Thalbiyath. After retiring from 'Umra' do 'Ihram' separately for Hajj.

Meekhaths

Separate places have been allotted to the pilgrims coming from different countries. These places are called Meekhaths. Yamlamlam is the place fixed for pilgrims coming from India, Java and Indonesia through Aden. Separate Meekhaths have been given for people going through other places. These are Dulhulaifa, Aljuhfa, Kharunulmanasil, Dathuirk etc. It is meant for people travelling through roadways. Now those who travel by Airplane go via Dulhulaifa.

Niyyathu

Before entering Meekhaths a center of revolution and great change, each Haji should declare his aim (Niyyathu). The aim is to shift from his house to the house of the people. That is changing from life to mercy, from him to Allah, from slavery to freedom, from racial discrimination to racial equality and truth. A change from extravagant dress to simple dress, from day to day life to eternity. In short a change to Islam.

He has to emphasize his purpose. Now we have perfect faith. So heart should be enlightened by love. Forget everything in the light. The former life was full of ignorance and negligence. He was helpless in all aspects. He worked like a slave. Give up the dull life and have knowledge about the Omnipotent Allah. Know yourself and the people. Find out a new job, a new direction and new identity.

It is said in the prayer at the time of preparing for Hajj that "Allah! I do not worship idols, not a slave of Nimrud. Allah! I am before you like Ibrahim, not as a torturer, a cheat, a corruptor, with the same dress when I see you in the other world, as a real man. I worship you alone. You alone give us mercy and help. You know we have gone astray from truth. Lead us to the right way, the path of your devotees, the path of truth, perfection, awareness, realty and beauty. Not the way of blasphemies" Amen!

Ihram cloths

A pilgrim enters Umra or Hajj by the ritual Ihram. Men wear one simple dhoti and another one for covering. The cloths should not be stitched. It is better to wear white cloth. The dressing style of women is noble. The portions to be covered should be covered. Women should not cover face. Cutting nail, trim moustache, bathing, comb beard and hair use perfume are sunnath before entering Ihram. After that should not cut nails, or remove hair on the body. Contact between husband and wife, kissing, touching with lust, etc. should not be done. If contact is made between husband and wife, Hajj is in vain. Give penance, tell no lies, make no quarrel, do no criminal acts, etc are strict

After any Namaskar or Sunnath enter Ihram. After these 'Labbaikka lil Hajj' (I enter in Hajj) so declaring 'Labbaikk Allahumma Labbaikka Labbaikk La shareeka lakka Labbaikk-Innalhamtha Va nniamatha Lakka Val mulk La shareeka lakka" (I come to your presence. My Lord! I am before you —I am before you —all glories, blessings and royalty are yours —no sharer to you). This is called Thalbiyath. It should be repeated loudly. When getting in a vehicle, going out, meet group of travelers, journey begins, it should be chanted loudly. It should be done until Hajj is over. Dedicating everything before the Lord, lakhs of people chant incessantly and loudly the devotional sentences and it goes beyond atmosphere and the sky is reverberated. Irrespective of religion, caste, race, poor, rich, white, black, lakhs of people have come before their Lord. This event will be repeated until the end of the world

Hajj begins from Meekhaths or points of entrance. Man has decided to return to Allah. His pride and selfishness are buried in Meekhaths. He becomes a witness to his dead body. He visits his grave. He is aware of his ultimate aim. He goes from Meekhaths to Mead.

This scene is like the Last Day. From a corner in the horizon a white army starts. All wore Kaffan (cloth on the dead body). None is identified. Their bodies have been left in the Meekhaths. They are now only inspired souls. None has name in this large crowd. Atmosphere of unity exists here. Man expresses the Oneness of Allah here.

In the magnetic field fear and joy are as tiny as atoms. Allah is in the middle of the place. Man is travelling to that aim. All sects of people join in the desert, become one clan and faces one 'Kaaba.' Clothes are removed and the identities as individual have been left. The individual becomes a part of human race. This is the state of Ihram (Hajj). All melt in to nothing in this stage. Finally one becomes everything. That is a society with Islamic leadership and having perfection, liveliness and straight forwardness.

Hajj begins from the eighth day in the month of Dulhaj. After doing everything as mentioned above, after Fajr Namaskar enter Hajj. Blowing Thalbiyath all go to Mena. It is a wide level ground four miles east to Mecca. It is in between Mecca and Arafa. After doing Luhar Namaskar they stay there singing prayer and hymns. On the 9th day after Fajr Namaskar and the Sunset, they set out to Arafa.

Hear the speech in the masjid at Nameeru and following the Imam of the masjid, do Namaskar in brief, Luhar and Assar in two Rekkaouth. There after be engaged in prayers until Sunset. In the middle of Arafa there is Jabalul Rah math- (mountain of blessing). It was on this hill His majesty the Prophet made his historical farewell speech in Hijra Tenth year addressing lakhs of pilgrims. On the 9th of Dulhaj, after Sun set return from Arafa and reaches Musdalifa. There do Namaskar of Maarib three Rekkaouth and Isha two Rekkaouth together. They stay there one day. Most of the people are used to be immersed in prayer. Stay at Musdalifa is compulsory. If it is given up penance should be given. Before the tenth of Dulhaj get up before sunrise and do Namaskar 'Vithir' and 'Fajr' and set out to 'Masjidulharam.' There glorify Allah specially and pray to Him. It is said in Holy Qur'an (2:198). On the fixed spots for throwing stones, throw seven stones at the third spot saying 'Allah Akbar.' Sacrifice should be done on the day itself.

On the same day (Du:Haj10)after completing all the acts at Mina, return to Mecca and do walking between the hills, Kaaba Thouvaf, and Safa-marva(Saia). Then shave hair take off 'Ihram' and wear usual dress and use perfumes. With this Hajj deeds are completed. Return to Mina and stay there. While staying there for three days, throw seven stones chanting' Thakbir' towards the rocky pillars erected at Jamrathul Ulayi. After three days' stay at Mena and after throwing stones at Jamrathul 'Vustha', return to Mecca and cirrcumlocute seven times around the Kaaba' or do Thouvaf. With this all the functions of Hajj are completed. This circumlocution is called 'Thouvaf ul Vidaa'. After this we can return to our native place.

Sacrifice

It is the stage of evolution, purity of ideas, ultimate freedom and ultimate obedience. Every Haji imitates in Mina Ibrahim (A) who sacrificed his own son Ismail. Ismail is only a symbol. That is a blind and deaf symbol which weakens and prevents man from doing responsibilities. This is to be sacrificed.

Historical places in Medina are to be visited. To do Namaskar in the Mosque, Masjid Navabi is a virtuous act. Those who go for Hajj do it either before or after Hajj.

Arafa, Mas her, Mina

The journey to Arafa is to the east. We should stay there until the Sunset of 9th day. Then start from Arafa, spend sometimes at Mas her. Then stay for a long time in Mina, Stay there since the dawn of tenth day to twelfth day. Signals are provided for identifying the places.

These places are shelters on the way. Mina is the most important shelter. Stay there for three days. But it is not the aim of Hajji. Aim is Allah-Eternity. He is eternal, limitless. A journey without rest, in this journey Allah is the aim and direction. For man everything is transient and mortal. But man's movement continues; he has always direction." All things except Allah would perish (H.Q.28:88).

There is motion everywhere. A motion towards God the journey should end at a place. Hajj is a pilgrimage, a path to attain aim. In the journey there are three stages —Arafa: Knowledge Mas her: Sense and understanding, Mina: Love and faith. The last and the long interval is at

Mina. It enlightens hope, purity of thought and love. Love is the last stage. It comes only after knowledge and sense.

Kaaba circumlocution

Kaaba circumlocution begins from 'Hajr ul Asvad.' Raising two hands and chanting 'Bismillah Allah Akbar' (Begins in the name of Allah, Allah is great) begins it. It begins and ends before 'Hajr ul Asvad'-a black rock erected there as a signal for uniformity for starting and ending the function. So that unity and discipline can be made. 'Thouvaf' is to be done seven times. The first 3 circumlocution of men should be in a little speed. It begins from the left side. Chanting and glorifying His name it should be done. After seven times circumlocution, prostrate two 'Rekkaouth' behind Makhamu Ibrahim, near, Kaaba. This is Sunnath. Some rules and manners are to be observed when come near Kaaba for circumlocution. Have cleanliness of body, cover nakedness, put the two tips of second cloth on the left shoulder and should have fear and respect (Our Lord! Save us from the punishment of Hell and give us goodness in the world and the other world). The Prophet used to pray while doing circumlocution. It is recorded by Abudavud.)

Every pilgrim should remember that it is the first worshipping centre for worshipping Allah and its historical background. The sacrifices of Ibrahim and the prayers behind it should be in mind.

Hajj is the annual conference of world Muslims. They are introduced one another. A group of people coming from different countries talking multi languages and wearing different dresses and in different color come together as believers in one religion and accept equality and fraternity as guide lines and work together for the welfare of the individual and the community. This is the message of Hajj.

'Thouvaf' has a philosophical aspect. An ecstatic crowd moves round Kaaba, like water current around a rock. It is like Sun in the Zodiac. People are the stars moving in their orbits. Kaaba stands for the eternity and constancy of Allah. His creations are always changing and inconstant like the pilgrims moving around Kaaba.

Those who do Hajj do not touch Kaaba. Every one moves around the circle, no difference of man or woman. All 'I' becomes 'We.' Allah becomes Truth. While doing thouvaf do not touch Kaaba or stand. Enter the crowd and disappear. Each and every one is absorbed and becomes Haji. Kaaba remains motionless in the middle. White- great- river flowing around; all are in the same dress, no difference, no peculiarities. It expresses unity and universality. That is the aim of Thouvaf. When go around Kaaba seven times, Thouvaf ends. It reminds us of seven Heaven.

Kaaba

It means prism. It is a simple arrangement of black, rough stones and white lime pasted in the gaps and the inside is empty rectangular; a rectangular with empty inside. It is neither a palatial building with architectural beauty nor a tomb erected over a great man. No grace or fair craftsmanship displayed in it. Here there is no graves no object or man to concentrate on.

Here is nothing to distract attention. Kaaba is the roof of the emotions of Hajji. There is some thing here which cannot be attained in this world of inconstancy. Now we can see Oneness here. A power without directions-Allah—He is everywhere. It is good. Kaaba is empty. We came here only for Hajj. It is not the aim. It is only a guideline. It is only a foundation stone, a guide.

The decision to do Hajj is meant to travel towards eternity. It is a move to Allah not to Kaaba. It is only a beginning, not the end, a place where Allah, Ibrahim and Mohammad join. We can reach there with a mind free from thoughts about the self. Be one of the people and wear simple dress. Now Hajji is a family and Kabba family of people. Allah says, No doubt, the first Mosque built for man is in Mecca. It is built as a blessed one and a guide to all people."(H.Q.3:96).

The meaning of Kaaba is prism. Why it has no ornamentation and splendor, because there is no form or color equal to Allah. No form or picture man can imagine has resemblance to Allah. He is Omnipotent Omnipresent.

Though it has no direction when we pry turning to Kaaba, we aim at Allah. It may seem to be obscure. The form prism points out the universality and Oneness of Allah. Prism has six sides. It represents all directions. When all directions are joined together, it loses direction. Kaaba is the first symbol of this concept. "East and West are to Allah. Where ever you turn there is the face of Allah."(H.Q.2:115).When we prostrate outside Kaaba, we face it. Every building turns either to east west south or north. Kaaba turns to all directions, but not turned to any. So it is the symbol of Allah.

There is a semi circular wall to the west of Kaaba. It was here Ismail lived. The house of Hajra was here. In between Hajr- Ismail and Kaaba there is a narrow path. If go along that way Thouvaf is not acceptable. Allah says that we should go round the wall when run around Kaaba. All who believe in One God and those who have accepted the invitation of Allah should revolve the wall during Thouvaf.

Those who do Hajj so, turns his face to Allah. He becomes blessed due to the mercy of Allah.

He enters a new stage in his journey. He faces ultimate realities. He overcomes oppression and ignorance. He gets sense, light and justice. He accepts Monotheism by denying Polytheism. Before Hajj, their generosity was neglected by others. They were affected by Wealth, family, power and dynasty. Their purpose of life was to do nothing. But experience of Hajj enabled them for self- realization. Now they understand each other.

Hajr ul Asvad

The word meaning is 'black stone'. There is no statement about its holiness or historical background either in the Qur'an or 'Hades.' There are many references about it in the Bible and other stories. The legend is that it is a rock slipped down from the Zodiac or brought it from Heaven. It is the first rock used for the holy house to worship Allah (Foundation stone). Once it had been damaged Abraham reconstructed it and he must have erected it in a particular point. It is a God house. Every part of it is holy. The circumlocution begins by touching it and ends near it. It shows the significance of foundation stone. However there are only some legends glorify its greatness. Qur'an does not command either to worship it or touch it respectfully two Sahabis (friends) Umar(R) and Ibnu Umar (R) recorded in two ways in Sahihul Bukhari. In the 26th chapter Hajj the sentence 782 says thus: Umar kissing it said. "You are only a stone. You are not able to do any good or harm to man. If I had not seen God's messenger kissing you, I would not have kissed you." Ibnu Umar says in the 26th chapter in the sentence 786 "WhenYour majesty came in Mecca he touched Hajr ul Asvad with his hand and found him doing thouvaf in hurry on the first three of seven thouvaf." So recorded differently by two people. In the Hajj classes it is said that after touching Hajr ul Asvad kiss the hand. But Ibnu Umar says it as "after touching with hand" and not kissing. To kiss a thing on the floor we have to bow head or lie on the ground. It is impossible to do it in large crowd. Kissing is an expression of joy not worshipping. There is nothing wrong in kissing.

Ibnu Umar said that His Excellency did Thouvaf by touching Hajr ul Asvad. It is true. To complete a circle it should end at the point where it started. If the point where Thouvaf begins is Hajr ul Asvad it should end there itself. As did by the Prophet, either kiss or touch in Hajr ul Asvad. But most of the Hajis kiss it. To do what is done by the Prophet is Sunnath. Do not do what he has not done. When touch the rock and kiss, the ignorant people are likely to fall in to idol worship. Give no undue importance to it. It may be mistaken as visible God.

There is description about fake hades in Bukhari when the world fell in the influence of Islam many joined it for selfish interests, not by mind, only in form. Many of had hatred towards the new faith and devotion to their religion. Many reasons are there. They presented their old religious principles in the form of Hades. For example, if one has faith in idols, he should be benefitted. It is imposed by the Prophet's rival and an idol worshipper who is totally against Islam" (Sahih Bukhari p162). "See, whether one Hades is anti to the fundamental principles and statements of Qur'an. If it is against, know that it is not the Hades of the Prophet" (Sahih Bukhari p: 163).

Qur'an does not say anything about the Prophet's kissing of Hajr ul Asvad. Qur'an which teaches us that 'Allah is one, free, not born, non- created and none equal to Him', does not permit to kiss or touch a stone at the time of Hajj. Allah is formless and omnipresent. Even to look at in a mood of reverence towards Hajr ul Asvad is an irony.

Qur'an strictly prohibits idol worship. Hajr ul Asvad is regarded as a stone brought from Heaven by Adam or fell from the Zodiac. Qur'an does not order to worship a stone in addition to Allah. The basic faith of a Muslim is that there is none except Allah. Idol worship was in the Kaaba temple where there were many idols. Does the Prophet of Islam who opposes idol worship permit to worship or respect a stone?

Stones are likely to fall from the Zodiac. When stars explode meteors may fall down to earth. Qur'an never says to worship these stones. If it is brought down from Heaven is not Allah who created the Prophet and Heaven to be worshipped. Does He bring a stone for worship? Hajr ul Asvad is erected in a corner as a signal to begin and end Thouvaf (Circumlocution). Every part of God's house is holy and sacred. But it is not permitted to worship its pillars, doors and walls.

It is commanded in the Qur'an to worship a power that pervades the entire universe, protects and destroys in the name of Allah. Thalbiyath chanting at the time of Hajj makes it very clear "Allah! I answer to your call. None is a sharer of your powers and rights. Allah! I answer to your call. All glories are to you. All blessings and supremacy are in your hands. None has share in your rights and power." Such monotheism will never allow idol worship (the act of touch and kiss a noble stone).

Hajr ul Asvad is only a signal for uniformity to start and end Thouvaf from a particular point. As not ordered we cannot worship it. "The East and the West belong to Allah. Where ever you turn Allah's face is there" (H.Q.2:115). It orders to all Muslims to turn their faces to Kiblah. It is not because these are visible Gods, but when from all directions faces are turned to Kiblah, the noble idea of unity and fraternity are included a good opportunity for them avoiding hatred and enmity. If possible when begins Thouvaf either kiss or extend right hand towards Hajr ul Asvad and do circumlocution. Worshipping Kiblah and Hajr ul Asvad are against Monotheism.

There is a philosophical aspect in saying that at the time of circumlocution the right hand should either touch or to be extended towards the black stone. This rock is a symbol of hand. That is the right hand of Allah. In ancient times individuals and leaders of clans were used to make agreements. It is to ensure safety in the desert. It is called 'declaration of solidarity'. It is done by one man holding the right hand of other one. That means that all the former agreements have been cancelled.

We choose our path and future near the black stone. Holding the right hand of Allah he agrees to become His follower and he is free from the former agreements. Thus now Hajjis are free from leaders of clans, the group of Khuraishi land lords and wealth. Holy Qur'an makes it clear that "the hands of Allah are above their hands" (H.Q.48:10).

Chapter 9
Informative Qur'an

All the contents of Qur'an have been narrated in the first chapter called 'Al Fathiha.' Qur'an says how to follow right path and reach the presence of Allah. "Those who obey Allah and his messenger are with those who have been blessed by Him, Prophets, martyrs, true men and good people. What a noble comrade! That is the bounty from Allah, and sufficient is Allah as knower." (H.Q.4:69-70).

This is to understand when a comparative study about religious texts are made —All the important religions in the world like, Islam, Christianity, Budhism, Hinduism, Jewism, Zorastrianism and Confucianism have religious texts. It is the source of principles. Among these Texts only Qur'an claims to be the words of the Lord of the Universe. It is Mohammad (S.A.) who presented Qur'an via the system 'Vahye.' It means the system by which God's message is brought to the Prophet through the angel Gabriel. Other religious texts do not place such arguments. Since the origin of all religion is the Creator, deletions or additions must have entered in the texts of other religions. These may be re written through the memories of prominent followers of the religion.

It is only Qur'an which has been received in real form, active and progressed. The other religions have been confined to mere translations and exist in obsolete languages. Qur'an written in Arabic language exists as pure literature in the world. It is difficult to deny the influence of Monotheism of Islam on other religions. It is the spiritual need of man just like water, air and light.

The study of Qur'an, Prophetic discipline and its practicability elevate man to a safe and noble height of spiritual culture. It leads man to a life without worries and troubles and in course of time, he becomes discouraged of Sanyasm and the establishments like Matt.

Holy Texts are handed down to man through Prophets by the Creator. Man has always received messages either as Holy Texts or Scriptures. 'Inchil' (The Bible) given to Jesus, Thora (Old Testament) given through Moses and 'Sabur'given through 'David' are such texts. Qur'an recognizes all other former Texts. The power that sent these alone can send it too. Qur'an said "nobody can write it except Allah. It approves and explains the former one. No doubt it is from the Cosmic Protector" (H.Q10:37). It has been ordered to the followers of Qur'an that all the Prophets and Holy Texts before Mohammed(Sa) should be recognized and accept them as prophets. "True believers you believe in Allah, His Prophets, the Holy Texts presented by Him and the Holy Text presented before that" (H.Q.4:136). "Make no distinction among His prophets" (H.Q.2:285). It means that the message of everyone was the same.

Noble status has been attributed to knowledge in Qur'an. What is presented more in it are the methods of reading and writing and how to earn and keep up the knowledge already earned. In the chapter 'Albakhara' 'the importance of knowledge is pointed out. These statements make it clear that man can live peacefully in the world by earning knowledge and he has got the ability to do so. At the same time man makes troubles and problems in the world and it often resulted in bloodshed. The statements 25 and 28 in the 35th chapter throw light on the fact that those who fear God really are learned people. The references of knowledge referred to in Qur'an are now called as science in the modern world.

Knowledge referred to in Qur'an is in one form. There is no difference in the branches like science, arts, subtle knowledge, or gross knowledge. Laws of nature implemented by the Creator, the activities of the animate and inanimate beings and the events that take place in man, society and the world due to the deeds on the basis of the rules, are the contents found in Qur'an. Qur'an says that all knowledge is subtle and deep. In Qur'an all knowledge is science. The word 'Ilmu' is used to refer to knowledge in Qur'an. Collect knowledge, understand reality, and live in the light of the earned knowledge and make life comfortable and cheerful. This is the aim of earning knowledge according to Qur'an. It is revealed in the 20th statement in the 31st chapter that man gets knowledge of God from the Prophet and Nature and God's blessings have been showered on man and everything in the sky and on the earth are bound by one rule and law This knowledge is useful to understand the Creator.

The Universe is opened before man like a book and he is asked to learn and do researches on it. H.Q67:3-4says "Seven skies are created in layers. Do you see any discrimination in it? You turn your face and look at it again and again! Eyes will return desperate; it may become exhausted, sure." Man is bound to learn and practice it. Those who do not do it are despised. H.Q. says many evidences are in the sky and on the earth. They pass by near them. But they neglect it. Qur'an says that, "those who understand the Creator and His creations through scientific studies have real devotion in God" (H.Q.35:27-28). "See you not Allah make rain from the sky? By that we produce multi colored fruits-different colored men, animals and cattle. Sure, among the servants of God, only the learned are afraid of Him"-these statements persuade man to earn knowledge in different branches of life. The Creator is beyond the studies, imagination and conclusions of man. Prophet says so, 'You think and study about the creations of Allah. Do not think of Allah, because you cannot calculate His greatness.'

Every thing in the universe is created, protected and destroyed by the laws of the Creator. It is called universal laws. But man alone has special laws to be obeyed or neglected-religious rules. These too, like the laws of nature, are changeless. "So being innocent, turn your face to religion! To that nature in which He created man. No change to the creations of Allah. That is the only existing religion. But most people do not understand it. "(H.Q.30:30).The scientific method in the Qur'an is understandable to both the literate and the illiterate. Each of them can grasp it according to his ability and intelligence there is no technical or difficult usages. The aim of Qur'an is not to mould scientists, but to turn man's mind to scientific knowledge and grasp it. There are many such scientific references in the Qur'an. The following things can be understood from the references in Qur'an

(1) Knowledge is inevitable in human life.

(2) it helps us to understand the reality.

(3) It helps us to enjoy harmlessly the resources of life.

(4) It leads to peaceful life.

(5) Man is convinced that good and evil deeds are rewarded.

(6) Man understands the mercy and other virtues of God.

(7) Gets knowledge about life after death.

(8) Man is bound to better his life in the light of the knowledge he got.

(9) He is bound to be grateful to the Creator.

Thus Qur'an will exist as alight to humanity

The greatness of Qur'an has been recorded in Sahihul Bukhari. Prophet told' no Prophet is born who could not make a superhuman act to create faith in man. I got knowledge from Allah. So hope that I would be the man among the Prophets with most followers on the day of resurrection' (Chapter66). Us man (R) says your majesty (S.A.) told 'the condition of one who has studied Qur'an by heart is like a camel. If it is always well protected, it is in control. If let loose, it will go astray'. Ibnu Masood (Ra) says your majesty (S.A.) told ' if any one of you say I forgot certain ayaths or sentences it is not fair. Let them say forgetfulness happened'. You renew memory about Qur'an. Qur'an will run away from the hearts of man in more speed than the cattle that run leaving the owners. Abumusa (Ra) says your majesty (S.A.) told 'The condition of a true believer who reads and practices according to it is like a lemon. Its taste and smell are pleasant. The condition of those who live according to Qur'an without reading is like dates. It has taste, but no smell. The condition of non- believers who read Qur'an, is like the spicy plant rayihan. Its fragrance is very good, taste is bitter. The condition of fake believer who does not read Qur'an is like attanga. Its taste and smell are unpleasant.'

Chapter 10
Shariath

Law is as old as man. As a social being man has to live in the company of others. Such contacts make quarrels and friendships. So the rights and duties of man are to be decided. The need of law arises there. When family came into being the word of the head of the family was the law. The society progressed. The head of clan became the law maker. When states came into being all the laws and rules of families and clans were unified and general laws were made. The laws of a country became different from another one. Later many reforms were made with the growth and change in views of life. Shariath is different from other laws. It is connected with Namaskar Vow zakat and faith in the other world of man and the matters of this worldly life. It is not molded by reforms of man who underwent many changes. It is presented by the Prophet in 23 years in practical ways for the people of all ages and countries. It is Islamic law. 'Shariath' ends with conditions to make rules for the needs benefits of the growing society as per the needs of changing and progressive society. The source of 'Shariath' is not man but the Creator of the Universe. Manmade laws are subjected to changes. But 'Shariath' needs no changes. "No change in the words of Allah" (H.Q.10:64).

Holy Qur'an is the important bas of 'Islamic-Shariath'. But the practices and traditions of Jahiliya (ignorant) period had been changed into social laws. They had strictly observed rules in economic fields like agriculture, trade and pledge. For example, burial of living girls, temporary marriage uncontrolled divorce, polygamy denial of wealth to women and children, were permitted. Traditional judges and approved laws were there to make judgments in the issues among people. Some of these insensible laws were totally weakened and reforms made.

The time of birth of Holy Qur'an is the twenty three years of life of the Prophet. This includes His 13years of life in Mecca and 10 years of life in Medina. The foundation of Islamic rules of this period was Holy Qur'an and Prophet's interpretations to it. The formation of social rules and perfection of Shariath are in the period at Medina. All the rules in Shariath are implemented as per the growth of Muslim society and its requirements. The system of law implemented by the Prophet in practicing Qur'an principles is Shariath itself. For example the amount affecting zakat and the amount to be given and conditions can be seen only through Hades.

Laws of Nature have been given to all creations by the Cosmic Creator. Birth, death, growth survival and all such states happen according to His Will. "He gives birth to all things and shows means" (H.Q.20:50). Allah has given special laws to man who has intelligence and wisdom. By observing these laws man can attain all eternal fortunes in the life after death and contentment. Peace and progress in the physical world. Allah has sent Prophets to send these principles to the people in every age. The collection of these divine laws is called Shariath or way of God.

The Creator alone can frame rules to satisfy the needs of man because He alone knows the needs and changes of the growing man. So Allah alone has the right to frame laws containing orders and prohibitions." the power of judgment is only to Allah."(H.Q.6:57). "Shariath has been implemented to you. You follow it. Do not go after the interests of the ignorant people" (H.Q.45:18). Since Shariath is God's law, man has no right to frame laws against it.' Do not obey anyone against the orders of the Creator.' (Hades)We obey rulers as the implementers of divine laws.

Three principles individual refinement, doing justice, and protection of interest, have been maintained. Kindness towards people is the aim of Islam. "You (Mohammad) are sent as kindness to the people of the world" (H.Q.21:107). The systems of worship give religious culture to people and it becomes beneficial to the society. For example, Namaskar purifies man from evil thoughts and deeds and it persuades him to live in harmony with others. Social sense and refinement involved in zakat Vow and Hajj are very clear. Doing justice is strictly observed in Islam. Justice should be displayed Laws, judgments and contact with others.

"Hatred towards one sect of people should not tempt you to be unjust. You show justice. That is the nearest way to devotion." (H.Q.5:9). Social justice should be observed in full sense, Islam exhorts. All are equal before law. Wealth, color and races should not be a bar for justice. Man is regarded as the respectable creation so religious difference is not a reason for violating human consideration or social sense of man. Islam denies such things. Social justice should be shown to all alike in his work freedom and enjoying the reward of work. Religion considers it a social duty to help the poor and be loyal to them in their rights.

Shariath judgments

The deeds of man are categorized into five in Islamic view.

(1) Compulsory things
(2) Prohibited
(3) Preferable to do
(4) Not preferable
(5) Freedom to do or not to do.

These are Wa jib (Furze) Haram Man dub Makruh Mubah

(1) Wa jib

What the religion says to be done compulsorily. If practiced well we will get noble reward from God or will get punishment. Namaskar, Vow, zakat, Obedience towards parents are included in it. Technically it is called 'Furze'. The deeds that make perfect all the loyalties of man are called 'Wa jib Kifai'- defense advice of morality, burial are included in it. If none does his social duty, all are guilty. Those who fulfill social duties must be given support. Scholars doctors farmers merchants judges are the requirements of each society. Each individual should do his duty to the society within his ability and limit

(2) Man dub

The deeds done of his own accord are called Man dub. Sunnath Nafilath Musthahaba and Ihsan are technical terms used to refer it. Generally Sunnath is partly compulsory and partly a need. So it should not be given up by people.

(3) Haram

Religion insists that certain things should not be done. Drinking liquor, prostitution, murder, theft and doing harm to others are included in it. Any thing which is related to interest is prohibited by the religion. Even if your deed is pure, if the situation is Haram, the deed also will become haram. Though sale is permissible, if done at the prayer time, it is prohibited.

(4) Makruh

The things religion demands without insistence are called Makruh. Violation of it is not punishable. But it is better to avoid it as disliked by the religion. It is divided into two 'Kara hath- Tah rim' 'Kara hath Thansih.' For example, do not use excess water.

(5) Mubah

The things man can do or give up according to his will are called 'Mubah.' Whether do it or not, no special benefit out of it. In the sense permissible, the terms Halal and Jays are used. It is not a Haram. No evidences that it is guilty. An example from Qur'an, "Dead body, Blood, Pork and the flesh cut without uttering the name of Allah are Haram. But if any one is forced to eat it in limit and without wish he is not guilty. All good things are permissible or Halal The food of those who presented Holy Texts is permissible" (H.Q.2:172). There is neither sin nor virtue by doing Mubah.

(6) Sarthe

The thing which stands as an initiative for implementing law is called Sarthe. For example, if Namaskar is to be proper 'Vulu' is necessary. If marriage is to be proper two witnesses are needed. Anything that acts as a reason for implementing law is 'Subahu.' For example in emergency eating dead body is permissible. Travelling becomes a cause for giving up Vow.

(7) Sahih

When Namaskar is done observing all details, it becomes Sahih. If financial transactions are to be proper, conditions should be satisfied. The things conducted violating procedure and rules are called 'Fasid' or 'Bathils.'

(8) Ijithihad

Utilizing ability for materializing a thing is called so. To utilize ability to find out religious judgments by examining records is called

Ijithihad according to Islam. It is the third important law in Islam. It is the method for finding out solutions to problems which rise up in new situations. When society faces a difficult situation first look into the Qur'an for a solution, if not found in it 'Sunnathu' should be applied. Then look for the unanimous opinion of Sahabis or examine similar situations or evidences and form an opinion for the welfare of man. It is a general commitment to find out answers for social problems

(9) Ijmaa

The third basic principle in Islam is Ijmaa. It means 'unity' or 'uniformity.' After the death of the Prophet caliphs were used to meet and discuss general issues If they arrive at uniformity of opinion the judgment will be executed. This is the basis of Ijmaa. It is the opinion of the scholars and not the society

(10) Khiyas

When Islam developed and spread in many countries and new states, situations arose, new issues came into being. The laws to solve these problems were not in the Qur'an and the scholars were constrained to seek remedies on the base of wisdom logic and justice. So they made new laws and principles and is called as 'Khiyas.' But it is not applied in Namaskar and Hajj. Man has no knowledge to frame laws based on systems of worship, though it is logical. If differences of opinion exist Khiyas can be applied in judgments. Laws cannot contain all situations and events, however deep it is. Sahrasthani says. "Records will be completed. But events have no end. When new situations arise, we should find out new laws applicable to it."

Chapter 11
Social life

Character formation takes place in the early stages of his birth. "Allah does not impose responsibilities and loyalties beyond his ability" (H.Q.2:286). Islam is a model and pragmatic religion. So it forgives human weaknesses. It is ready to forgive when man slips down into errors quite inadvertently. The errors in deeds can be corrected. "So if any one of you do wrongs by ignorance and corrects it later after repentance, know that Allah is a forgiver and a kind one."(H.Q.6:54). But if one deliberately denies truth and does as he likes his deeds are in vain, it will lead him to discontentment.-This is what an ignorant man does.

Islam enables man to lead a multi faced social life. It criticizes solitary life and separation. Islam invites man not for executing his duties alone, but to enjoy his rights. That is a social life which is a blend of idealism and realism. He is bound to all layers of human nature and expression of freedom is given much importance.

By nature the whole universe obeys the Creator. But man alone obeys Him according to his will, because man is blessed by willpower and wisdom. So he is responsible for his character. We can see soul, knowledge and expression of ideas in all the things in nature. So they have a life of their own. Qur'an invites man to study nature and show mercy and lively interest towards it, because everything lives with same purpose and aim.

Islam is very practical in its approach to man. It is generous and compromising towards man. Even though man cannot show generous attitude to others, he should control it. Do not react in anger.

It agrees with tolerance, power and opportunity for revenge. But it should not be mixed with cowardice or helpless surrender. Man should prepare himself for self-defense. He should be safe from suppression. He should acquire power.

As Islam is the religion of generosity, a part of expense is for others and describes how much it should be. It emphasizes the need of generous distribution in order to eradicate economic difficulties and implement social welfare. Charity should begin from home Gifts are to be given first to parents, relatives, poor devotees and to all the needy. It should be done without considering caste or faith. Donations can be given either in secret or in public. That depends upon situation. It is not for displaying one's pride or egoism. It orders to all of its followers friends and parents to be unselfish and kind to all for the peaceful existence of the society. We should have love, sympathy and service towards all. Love and respect towards parents comes next to God worship in Islam. "Be grateful to me and to your parents too" (H.Q.31:14). If worship is to be acceptable to God, we should be thankful to parents too. They should never tell to follow wrong religion. One has right to select his faith. The principles and courtesy of Islam are seen in the statement. "Help each other in goodness and devotion, but not in sin and violation of laws."(H.Q.5:2).

This is the natural way to resist the spreading of ill fame and evil in the society.

Islam has permitted up to four wives, if proper care and protection can be given. It is not compulsory. On the basis of ideal love this trend can be criticized. In the lacking of this right lavish sexual freedom and the resultant social issues and unrighteous behavior towards women cannot be neglected.

Islam does not evade from realities of life. It accepts things as such and tries to accommodate in practical ways. It stands fixed in the ideology that is based on reality.

It neither suppresses nor destroys human nature. On the contrary, it controls it. It acts as a guide to the natural growth. Islam is actual, realistic and then idealistic. If a religion is helpful to the growth of humanity it is good.

In general other religions are averse to material growth in the financial field. This is the essence of all the popular religions in the world. The followers get a chance to choose either devotion or spirituality. Islam aims both material and spiritual progress as the greatest relation in the world the Prophet encourages marriages. He threatens that disagreement with it will result in dismissal from it. The attitude of Islam towards the world is brave and acceptable and not shameful or renunciation. "This is no objection to enter water; but does not allow to drown; but to teach how to swim properly" said Mohammad Pickthal.

Considering the righteous and physical state, Islam believes that pork, liquors and wine are prohibited items. It is acceptable in Islamic countries. In the laws of progressive governments this law has real importance.

Islam is against amassing wealth by doing no work, and doubling it through illegal means. It strongly opposes Capitalist rules. It encourages combined business and its profits.

Lending and borrowing money is inevitable in a society. Islam stands for helping the needy. It permits the borrower to give some kind of gift to the lender as a token of gratitude. It is not interest, only a gift. Islam considers it as a matter of sympathy and gratefulness. By doing so peace and welfare will increase in society. Thinkers have admitted its greatness and understood the dangers caused by interest among people. Inequality in economic field resulted in poverty and as the result Socialism, Communism and Bolshevism came in to being.

Generally Communism and individual nobility stand face to face. The merits of one are the defects of the other. Considering both, Islam has presented law of property. No joint family system, no traditional ritual-a medium system which allows individual growth. By this the doer can enjoy the benefits of his work and thus property is distributed to the relatives through the law of property right via Communist theory. Islam compares property to a sea. At times its waves may go high. Later it will come down and spread along the shore alike.

Chapter 12
Islamic family life

Family is a small community. Humanity studied the noble social habits from family. Those who show enmity to family are the breakers of good traditions already built in many years. It is family which keeps and hands over the past achievements to the next generation. Qur'an says that the creation of family relation is God's blessing. "Your protector who created man from water and gave blood relation and marriage, is powerful" (H.Q.25:54). Married life is the basis of family.

We have to understand the Islamic view regarding the role of women in married life. When the Prophet began the teachings of Islamic religion, women were in a pitiable condition in many countries. They were subjected to tortures and suppressions of many kinds. Even the birth of a female child was regarded as a dishonor, Qur'an describes this condition in Arabia as "If the happy news that a female child is born, his face will become dark by grief. He suppresses grief and anger. Being unable to bear the disgrace of the unhappy news, he disappears. What is to be done to rear the child or burry her. Ha their fate is very pitiable!"(H.Q.16:58-59).

Islam has given unprecedented rights and powers to women that no religion, culture or law has recognized so far. Islam declared that man and woman are equal. "Man and woman are created form the same soul "Qur'an says. When some religions put the blame on the woman that she not only ate the forbidden fruit but tempted Adam to eat it, Islam purifies both from the sin. They said "Our Lord! We did wrong to ourselves. If you do not forgive and show mercy we will be losers." (H.Q.7:22).

Woman is the center for man to reach the state of peace. "A companion for you is created from you is His proof. For you to get peace through her" (H.Q.30:21). "Man is woman's dress and woman is man's dress."(H.Q.2:187) "Woman is from man and man is from woman" (H.Q. (3:195). She can reach the heights of glory through virtuous deeds. "Whether man or woman, whoever do noble deeds, their deeds will not be made in vain by me" H.Q. (3:195).To all—Muslims men and women true believers, men or women, honest and dishonest, righteous or unrighteous, the patient or impatient people who take vow or no vow those who keep up their sexual organs and those who remember Allah, Allah has arranged redemption from sin and noble rewards." (H.Q33:35).

Islam has permitted freedom to all women who had experienced slavery. Education is permitted to women. She is free to conduct business and transactions in finance. She is free to be witnesses in the court and has permission to be judges to make judgments for men and women, she is told to have her own role in army. The woman, Ummu Athiyya said 'I took part in seven wars along with the Prophet. My duty was to nurse the wounded, and the patients, and to watch the belongings of the soldiers' (Hades). Ummulkhair, Ummu sinal, Sarkha Akras and Khusaima are brave women who took part in war and served as commanders.

She has freedom to criticize the rulers and it should be paid attention. When Omar made a law forbidding gifts at the time of marriage was questioned by a woman quoting from the Qur'an, soon Omar withdrew the order. She can even take up party leadership. She has freedom to take part in the group prayer conducted in the Mosque for five times and the prayer on Friday (Juma). It is a noble deed to women too. "If wife asked permission to go to Mosque, do not prevent it": Prophet said. Hades says that women had come to the Mosque even in darkness for morning - prayer. Prophet stated clearly the manners to be observed in the mosque. "We are asked to bring all ladies including menstruated-women and girls to the masjid on the day of, 'Id ul Fithir', and 'Id ul Azha.'

But menstruated women should keep away from Namaskar and they can take part in other virtuous deeds. (Muslim).

She is exempted from the difficulties of earning money, physical work and liabilities relating to it. She is given all kinds of freedom and rights of men. The liability of protecting women is with man. Home care and child protection should be done by woman. She is not prohibited from doing any job she likes, if it does not affect her family life. Reasonable property of family share has been permitted to woman by Islam. Really high status has been given to woman by Islam.

It is argued that giving half of the property right to woman is a sign of attributing low status to her. According to Qur'anic law man has double share of woman's property. It shows respect towards woman. Really, she has no right to have equal share of man, because all her expenses are met by man. Rarely a woman is forced to take up liabilities of a family. In all stages of life—wife, mother, sister, daughter, man is obliged to look after her, so double share to woman's property should be given to man. That is just and reasonable. Islamic religion has taken precautions that woman should not be exploited on any account. What a woman needs is respect and love and not sympathy. Gentlemen alone will respect her. Evil minded people despise her for no reason.

Chapter 13
Marriage and Divorce

The sacredness attributed to marriage according to Islamic rule has not been fully grasped or appreciated.

It is said in the text, 'Ash bah va Anna sair.' It is ordered to the safety of humanity and to safeguard oneself from violation of chastity." Marriage is a holy act of worship to keep mankind from pollution. 'It is set up by God. It is a contract based on mutual agreement from the man and the woman. It is a strong relation which is not against legal union. Holy Qur'an makes it clear "woman has got strong contract from you" (H.Q.4:21). It is the most important contract a man is obliged to keep up. Prophet says "The contract you made to make relation between man and woman legal is one you are bound to keep most."(Bukhari).

It is a legal relation between man and woman. It is a sacred contract in Islam. The bridegroom in person and guardian representing the bride take part in it. The marriage is conducted in public in the presence of two witnesses. The gift given by the man to the woman at the time of wedding is called 'Maher.' It may be anything costly. In the days of Prophet, teaching Qur'an was regarded as a Maher to the poor people. "I give my daughter in marriage to you" says the father in public, "I accept it" says the bridegroom. It is the formality of marriage. Though it is the duty of finding out the bridegroom is for the parents, without permission and contentment of the bride marriage cannot be conducted. She should be consulted about her marriage. Her silence is the sign of agreement. She has right to seek legal means to make invalid the marriage conducted without her consent. Perfect unity between man and woman is a must for a successful married life.

Allah unites man and woman through marriage. Thereafter each of them is called 'companion'. They were separate individuals before marriage. They represent each other and share joys and sorrows. The word husband means one who rules. Wife means one who is ruled. These words are quite alien to Qur'an. The Qur'anic usage 'zauj' or companion represents a high level of status.

Control and discipline are necessary for the perfection of sexual passions. Every one except the anarchists agrees to it. Rarely even they agree. Marriage is a noble affair which gives social approval to sexual relation and family life. It is strictly religious and Godly. Even atheists and blasphemers understand and practice it in their life, so illegal connections of any kind treated with contempt even those who do it. Family is the smallest unit in a society. It is formed through marriage. Disagreements in married life will certainly create disharmony tension and unrest in life. For a healthy and peaceful life a secured and safe married life is a must.

The views of married life put forward by Islam are entirely different from the criterion of mathematics. In Mathematics one plus one is two. Islam teaches that one plus one is 'a big one.' Like two rivers join as one, two lives are joined as one. It is a wonderful and indescribable phenomenon and that is why Qur'an qualifies "man as the dress of woman and vice versa" (H.Q.2:187). Qur'an says "foundation of marriage is love, mercy and affection"(H.Q.30:21). Man is prepared to dedicate everything for love. Matured love grows. Love should be based on mutual understanding and humanitarian consideration. It helps man and woman to forget and forgive the faults of the other one. It enables one to solve any problem easily and to live happily.

Islam has clearly stated how to behave to woman. "You behave very decently to woman (H.Q.4:19).Women are the 'amanath' (entrusted) dedicated in man. Prophet in his farewell speech said, "In the case of women you listen to Allah. 'They are dedicated in you as the Amanath of Allah' (Thirmidi). Religion has permitted to decide the ways of behavior towards women as per the changes in situations. Still she should be given all the comforts and enjoyments that a man enjoys. In married life the rights of man and woman are equal." They have rights corresponding to their liability"(H.Q.2:228). The duties of man and woman in family has been divided by Islam. Even though they are equal in rights, a leader of family is necessary for safety and security strong shoulders to carry the burden of family life is a must. Since man has more powerful hands and body man is the head of the family. But child care and family rule are invested in woman. But she is fragile in compared with man. They should not be tortured. "Do not trouble them for suffering." (H.Q.65:6).

In the view of Islam marriage is immortal. With dreams sweet hopes and intense joy we enter the garden of marriage. But dreams may not be fulfilled always. Dreams are different from realities. With unfamiliar hopes we step into marriage. Sometimes they may stand against by petty quarrels which are very common. When people with varied taste, aptitude, ideas and ideologies join together, naturally differences may occur. It may be difference in views. At this Islam interferes. It helps couples to keep up mutual faith and trust in life. It keeps them away from being affected by scratches or damages in life. Islam takes care that the strong base of life receives no shock. It demands tolerance and patience from the couples. "If you are lenient and forgive patiently Allah is forgiving and merciful" (H.Q.64:14). Prophet (S.A.) said "No true believer should hate his wife. If one behavior of her displeases him another one will satisfy him" (Muslim).

No husband may be able to materialize all the dreams of his wife. Like wise his character, behavior and mannerisms may be different from her. Her fair face becomes dark and cheerless. Her cheeks grow dark and black due to anger. Husband also becomes tense and restless. His eyes grow red with anger. However all the displeasure on their faces should be wipe out. Islam reminded "woman who can endure the evils of her husband will get the great reward that Asiya the wife of Far ova gets" (words of Prophet).Man becomes angry when he sees unpleasant behavior in his wife, he loses control. His tongue goes beyond control. The flower of married life fades soon. So Prophet said, use no obscene words to wife" (A hammed, Abu davood).

Prophets' married life is a model in the world. He appears pleasant before his wives. Ayesha (Ra) says, "If he is alone with wife, he is a gentle smiling type of man." His greatness, responsibility or seriousness was not a bar for entertaining his wife. "You beat your wife during day time, at night lie with her. No shame to you?" Prophet said. "Woman is created with a curved back bone. The curve will never be straight. If you want to enjoy her do it with the curve. If try to straighten the curve you will break it" Prophet advises. Do household work to house wife is a gift. Prophet had shown it in his life. He had reminded of the seriousness of married life. "Each of you is a ruler. Each of you will be trialed about those under you. Man is the ruler among house members. He will be asked about the members. Woman is the ruler in her husband's house. She will be questioned about the members under her" (Bukhari).

Divorce

It is the result of misunderstanding and differences of opinion among the couples. Islam shows more sense of justice and consideration towards women than other laws. In ancient countries the power for divorce was a part of marriage laws. But it became beneficial to the rich classes in the society, except certain cases. Wife was on no account had the right for divorce. Growth of ideas and the progress of civilization led to some kind of comfort and relief in the case of women. They too got unconditional right for divorce. But this convenience for marriage and divorce became a satirical affair in the rule of Roman emperors. So men used it freely.

According to ancient Hebrew law a husband can give up his wife for any reason. There was nothing to prevent man's power to do so. But women were not permitted to get divorce from their husbands. Hillel laws or Hebrew laws existed in Arabia in the early days of the Prophet. Renunciation of women by their husbands was a common practice among them.

The authority of husbands for divorce among Arabs was unlimited. They showed no justice or consideration towards women in their behavior. They accepted no law which stood for woman. They contemptuously looked upon divorce as a practice which digs the foundation of the society. God prefers nothing more than to free slaves and nothing more unpleasant to him than divorce. Mohammad has stated so. It was impossible to abolish it completely as per the rules existed in the society. When time is ripe the spiritual awareness of man will increase and he will throw away uncultured and brutish practices. The mind of the society will develop. Rituals were always evils in some aspects. So He permitted some rights for conditional divorce to men. He permitted three regular and irregular periods for divorced parties. During this period they would try for compromise and reunion. When all attempts for reconciliation fail the last stage of separation comes. It is the third stage. Reconciliation through mediators is also entertained during this time.

In the law making of eastern countries the reforms of Prophet became a turning point and he controlled the authority of man for divorce. He gave right for divorce on the basis of reasonable causes. But towards the end of his life, he moved to the stage of prohibition instead of restriction. He declared that Thalak or divorce is a despicable affair to Allah because it is against the enjoyment of married life and an obstacle for rearing children carefully. So the consent given in the Qur'an is to be understood in the light of the explanation of the lawmaker. Law and religion have been very closely connected in Islamic theory. The gist of Prophet's words on divorce can be understood by us very clearly. Thalak from the part of the husband is really forbidden affair. But if it questions the chastity of the wife Thalak is allowed. Hanafi Maliki Shafi and majority of Shia consider Thalak permissible, even though the utilization without the interference of court. It is of his own accord a group of learned lawyers consider that Thalak as an authority is illegal.

What are the practical aspects of divorce? There may occur petty quarrels and issues which may create disharmony in life. Man differs in nature and character. Some women may quarrel for silly reasons. Retaliation is not a remedy. In contexts like this man should show more tolerance and maturity and advise her lovingly. Convince her of her faults and explain to her the after effects of evil habits. Tell her about the dangers of disobedience. "If women show disobedience advise them." (H.Q.4:31). A leader to the society, a ruler to the nation and a head to family, it is inevitable. As man is proportionately powerful Islam entrusts this responsibility with him. So he is bound to keep harmony and peace in family.

If advice fails, strong and fruitful methods are to be used. It is merely psychological. It is pretence of quarrel and lay separate them in the bed room. The ability of woman to charm man is challenged here. She understands that all her weapons fail before the will power and self control of her husband. She knows that there is no way except yield to him. So the second step to be shown towards woman is "keep away from women" (H.Q.4:34).

Endless disharmony may exist in spite of attempts to keep up peace and joy in the life. Quarrel may become powerful and mutual understanding is totally spoiled. Even then should not jump into the conclusion of divorce. Select mediators from each family to try for a compromise. The head of the family selects mediators.

An attempt for compromise is strict and compulsory. It is inevitable, Qur'an teaches. "If husband and wife think of divorce you engage one mediator from his side and another one from the woman's side. If both of them wish reconciliation, Allah will try for unity. Sure, Allah is keen and wise" (H.Q.4:35). In the absence of Islamic rule and courts, masjid and Quasis are to take the leadership for compromise.

Mediation failed. No chance for reunion. Both the parties are convinced of the danger. Marriage becomes not a relation but a prison to be separated soon. In such contexts, Islam permits divorce. The Prophet said "in permissible affairs divorce is the most unpleasant thing to Allah." "Allah has not permitted anything more angry than divorce" (Dara Khuthni). Ali (R.A.) said "You marry. Do not say Thalak or divorce because that may   shake even the throne of God" (Khur Thubi).

Repetition of marriage and divorce simply for the sake of enjoyment is sin. Prophets forbids it in harsh words. "You marry. Do not divorce her. Allah never likes man and woman who do it for enjoyment "(Dara khuthni).

Invalid Thalak or divorce

1) Done yielding to the compulsion of parents or relatives and not voluntarily

2) Divorce of the mad or liquor addicted

3) Divorce of the angry man who knows not what he says or does. Prophet says, "Release from slavery and Thalak are invalid when the mind is clouded" (Ahammad, Abudavud, Hakim and Ibnu Maja.)

4) Doing unconsciously or as a fun or by mistake it has no support of laws. So divorces in reasonable and sensible contexts are valid.

Prohibited stages

Divorce is really improper and prohibited. Abdullah Ibnu Abbas said: "divorce is only in inevitable circumstances." It would not be done in hurry. If all attempts fail proper opportunity should be chosen.

The most proper time for divorce is when the woman is free from menses. In this stage of cleanliness sexual contact should be avoided. Husband should keep aloof from wife at the period of delivery and menses. Even silly things will irritate husbands when sexual relation is prohibited. So it is asked to wait until she is clean and should be before making sexual contact with her. Divorce is forbidden during menses and the time of cleanliness after sexual contact. The benefit of this rule is that the decision of separation will be obstructed by pregnancy through sexual contact during the time of cleanliness.

If do not touch the woman when she is clean and get ready for divorce knowing she is pregnant, it is clear that the gap between them is unbridgeable. It is not the result of temporary grudge. In such contexts Thalak is permissible. Allah declares. "When you divorce a woman do Thalak at the time of her purity." Swearing and threatening that his wife will be divorced are forbidden things. So to say that 'if you do it, you will be divorced' is forbidden.

Witnesses

Two witnesses are required for divorce as in the case of marriage. Thalak is not one done in hurry in a weak point by in anger. So if divorce is decided do it in the presence of two witnesses who are just. Whether written or in words, Thalak is valid. Allah says "after when they get leave, receive them happily or separate decently. There should be two honest witnesses among you."

A divorced woman should stay in husband's house during 'Idda.' (waiting). Generally it is a period of completing three menses. "Divorced women have to wait until they have three times menses. They have no right to keep hidden what Allah has created in their womb, if they believe in Allah and Last Day" (H.Q.2:228).

One Idda is a period of cleanness of a woman after three menses. But in the case of pregnant woman it is up to delivery. "The period of Idda of pregnant woman is up to they deliver" (H.Q.65:6). The Idda period of women whose menses ended due to disease, old age is three months. "If you doubt about menses in the case of poor women, their Idda period is three months. It is the case with women without menses" (H.Q65:4). During the period of Idda she is not the wife as far as husband is concerned, but not a stranger.

A divorced woman should stay in the house where she lived before it. Husband has no right to send her out of the houses without sufficient reason and she has no right to go. Because husband has right and obligation to call back her to married life.

The woman in his house even after divorce gives husband a chance to think again. It will create lust and love in him towards her. He will think of ending separation. It is a time for examining whether she is pregnant. The sacredness of married - life is thus kept up in this period. During this time their anger will cool down and they will try to go back to the former days of joy and satisfaction. "Have an eye on your Allah. Do not dismiss the woman from the house where she stayed during Idda. They should not go out of their own accord but if they are involved in illegal relations, nothing wrong" (H.Q.65:1).

Islam strictly observes that if divorce is inevitable it should be done without unnecessary allegations, charges and violating the rights of one another. "You live decently with her or separate from her in noble manner" (H.Q.65:2). "Either keep her well or send her away decently" (H.Q.2:241).

He has right to take her back before the completion of Idda period. He has right to marry her again. When they return to life again and if hatred and disharmony grow between them, and all attempts for compromise fail, they can be divorced again. During the period of Idda, he can call her back to his life.

If divorce is made for the third time, it is sure that they can never be united. So after three divorces she has no right to take her back or marry her. The first husband can marry her only when she is married with a man and they are engaged in sexual relations. There after they are separated by passing through all the procedures as of old. Thus after the divorce, the first husband can marry her again. Allah says "If she is divorced for the third time, she is not permitted to him, until she accepts another husband. Later if he disconnects relations with her, nothing wrong if she and her former husband return to old relation, if they believe in the powers of Allah! It is God's limit. He describes it to those who understand it" (H.Q.2:230).

By this instruction Islam eradicated the evil practices that existed in Arabia before the advent of Islam. They had rights to divorce a woman countless times. So women subjected to indescribable kinds of tortures. Women could not escape from men or marry again. Qur'an was actually closing doors to an injustice done towards women. It denies right to take back the woman who is divorced three times. So it is a risk for the husband that he will lose his wife for ever.

Ayesha (R.A.) tells about the practices of Arabs "If man decides divorce he did it. If took back during the period of Idda she would become his wife. If divorced even for hundred times this was the condition." Once a man told to his wife "I won't avoid you by divorce, at the same time I won't take care of you." The woman enquired how was it? He replied: "I will say Thalak and before the completion of Idda will take you back. It will be repeated. She told it to Ayesha. She made no response until Prophet came. It was told to the Prophet. He quoted from the Qur'an "divorce is only for two times. After that live with her or send her decently" (H.Q.2:229).Those who do divorce for the second time should know that her chance is over.

Cursed practices

The three Thalak means divorces of three times. It is unlike what we see today. Now three Thalak are made together. This is really ridiculous and wicked. Prophet has criticized it harshly. When Prophet was informed that a man made Thalak in one word at a time. Prophet asked him "are you playing with Holy Text when I am among you?" Ibnu Abbas quotes, "Rukkanath divorced his wife and said Three Thalak in the very same place. Later he felt sorry for that was informed to the Prophet. Then he enquired "How did you say Thalak?" He answered "I said Thalak three Times." "Is it at the same place?" "Yes" replied he. "Then it is only one." So if you want you can take her back" (Hades).

Many scholars say that even if three Thalak are said together even one is impracticable because it is bad habit. "Bad habit is not a law" says Al Islam Val Athul Mu asra (page 117). Really the existing rule is that if three times are said only one will come into practice. Qur'an says so.

Many of the scholars comment that most of the divorces in the society are improper and unjust.

The lapses are due to the loopholes in the personal laws. It is true. So Muslim individual law is to be compiled as per the instructions of the Prophet and the Qur'an and it is inevitable.

Rights of divorced woman

A misunderstanding exists in society that with the telling of divorce sentence husband and wife become strangers, but as described above they stay together in husband's house during the Idda period. In those days protection of the woman is in the hands of the husband. He is bound to give food, clothes and all other things. If she is pregnant he is bound to carry the expense until delivery and the responsibility of the feeding child. Bad behavior is not allowed. Such a generous law stating that a divorced woman should be given all comforts in the husband's house for three months is only in Islam. Allah says "stay her where you stay. Do not harm her simply for troubling. If she is pregnant, carry out her expenses until her delivery. When she feeds your child give reward to her. If you dislike it, let another woman feed the child" (H.Q.65:6).

The time when calling back is permitted at the time of Idda if the wife dies husband will get the succession right and vice versa. The marriage gift given at the time of marriage is wife's right. It cannot be accepted back. "If you wish to accept another wife, avoiding the first, do not accept anything even if you have given a great share of your property. If you take it back by making allegations it is a clear sin"(H.Q.4:20). If the divorce is before touching wife, give only half of your property. Better to be generous. "Since marriage value has been fixed, if you divorce before making with her give a half of what you decided. If neither the man nor the woman shows leniency, better men should show generosity. Do not forget generosity among you. Allah sees everything you do."(H.Q.2:237)

If wedding value is not fixed early, man is not bound to give that. Still something reasonable should be given. "Before touching or divorcing her before fixing value you have no obligation to give Maher. But you should give something for her existence the rich or the poor according to their ability. It is the duty of virtuous people" (H.Q.2:236) .In contexts like this women need not observe Idda. "So give something and divorce her decently" (H.Q.33:49).

One should not take back women before 'Idda' in order to prevent her marriage by extending the Idda period. It is un-Islamic and a sin. Qur'an comments rudely, if you separate relation with woman and the time of Idda is nearing, make her stay well. Do not put her in your custody only for harming. That it is an insult to them. "Do not ridicule God's orders" (Hades).

After the period of Idda, husband or nobody has right to prevent the remarriage of her. No one has right to interfere in the interests of her well wisher. In the un- Islamic period of the Arabs the divorced man has tried to keep her in his control and to prevent her from remarriage. Islam strictly put a stop to it.

If the person who said Thalak (Two times) wishes to remarry the divorced woman and the differences between them are solved, relatives or patrons should not object it, should not do it in the name of pride and vanity. "If you divorce women (Two times) and their holidays come near if approved each other, do not object to them marrying of their former husbands; it is an order to those who believe in Allah and Last Day. This is the most useful and noble path for you, Allah knows. You do not understand it (H .Q. 2:232).

Really the most deserving one for remarriage is the former husband. "Their former husbands are the most deserving ones to take them back if they are ready to make their relationship better" (H.Q.2:228).

If there is no other alternative even after staying in husband's family for many days, it can be done. Only by expressing and wishing all blessings the man should bid farewell to her mate who lived with her for a long time enjoying the most precious and delightful moments in life. Islam says that the gifts would certainly reduce her tension to some extent. Allah says "divorced woman should be given resources for enjoyment. It is the liability of God believers" (H.Q.2:241).

Divorce due to silly reasons

Now even for silly reasons divorces take place among Muslims, even though Islam has strict and sacred rules of marriage and it hates separation. Really it is to be done only when all the doors are closed for living together Islam has no view that man should not separate what God joined. God made relation can be broken subjecting to the laws of God. Hatred and revenge in the family will result in complete breakdown of family life. It is better to escape from such a hell than suffering endlessly.

Marriage is really an emotional attachment to last until death between man and woman and a sacred contract to make each other happy and contented. It should not be weakened for silly reasons. Crisis and issues which may naturally arise should be solved by broadminded attitude and mutual love and respect. Petty quarrels on no account, would affect the smooth life of the couples. Separation is not a solution to be arrived at. Joy and hatred are short lived feelings which should disappear the next moment. Soon emotional ground divorce will not be done. Marriage is a spiritual affair. Tolerance and patience are needed for ensuring the safety and security of married life. The strength of society depends on the strength of family. So high status should be given to marriage as a divine relationship between two souls. The followers of Islam should try to be firm and strong in keeping up right understanding and love between couples.

Unfortunately Muslims are in a ridiculous state in this matter. Now in some places the bad practice exists among Muslims. As Qur'an demanded none follows the instructions for making compromises between the wife and husband. None cares for the instruction that divorced woman should stay in the house of husband during the Idda period. All are hurried to say the three Thalak together. It is against Islamic rule. Some wrong practices exist among Muslims and not the teachings of Qur'an.

In all other countries Muslim women have right to demand divorce. But in India it is denied. When British rule was set up the right of Indian Muslim women was taken away. But women can move to the court of law for divorce.

Chapter 14
The status of women in Islam

The social condition of Indian Muslim women is in a ridiculous state. It is due to the ignorance of the rights and freedom permitted by Shariath to Muslim women. The whole society has to suffer for it. So long has it exists, social decline, child death weak and fragile children, are the dangers the community has to endure incessantly. It is because of the deep rooted anti Islamic tradition born out of ignorance in the minds of majority of Muslims. It is has become a part of the subconscious mind of the common Muslims. Ignorance is not a reason to escape from punishment. Shariath laws are laws of nature if neglected it, no man will escape from the after effects of it. It is like playing with fire. The denial of Shariath is a sin to the Muslims. It is the duty of Muslim to study it and spread the messages among all kinds of people. "In some parts of India the condition of Muslims are more pitiable than scheduled tribes" Sachar committee reports so.

Holy Qur'an says "I have made you a middle class society so as to act as witnesses to human race, like wise Allah's messenger will be a witness to you" (H.Q.2:143). Sure the messenger of Allah is now against you in protecting the rights and status of women. These are the words of the Prophet: education is the sacred duty of each Muslim woman. Some influential people among Muslims have attributed restricted meaning to education. To them it means Theology. Holy Qur'an and the Prophet made no distinction between material and religious knowledge. To a real Muslim his whole life is religious. A learned and experienced man is the most competent one to interpret religion and find out remedies for issues regarding religious practices. But interference of Priests and interpretation of Qur'an spoiled the essence of real religious principles. That is the reason for the backwardness of Muslim community. Each Muslim woman should acquire religious knowledge along with formal education. Only then she can understand the progressive ideas of Qur'an about woman.

Prophet said: "woman is half of man." Her rights are sacred. We should see that their rights exist. Indian Muslim women are unaware of their rights. As per Shariath, equality is the right of women like that of men. They have claim over property. In certain circumstances, she can demand divorce. But however their rights have not been protected. Imam Abu Haneefa opines that a woman judge should be appointed in every town to handle the rights of women. Even though there are Women Protection Committees and National Women Commission, the scarcity of local judges, denies the chances of Muslim women to get their grievances redressed.

The faithless Arabic woman thought that woman is a low category. But Qur'an reminds all that all belong to one category and man and woman are created from one another. Blessings of nature like Sunlight, fresh air, and health are for all and so not denied to women. There is no word or sentences in the Qur'an exempting women from the rights of life.

The Prophet of Islam is perhaps the greatest man among the leaders of Woman Liberation Movement ever seen in the world. He raised the status of women to the highest level. She can go beyond it only by theories. The Arabs in his time looked upon woman with contempt and sarcasm. They were used to be cheated and ridiculed by them. Qur'an said: "None of you is permitted to become the heir of her property without her consent. If you hate them, you behave kindly towards them, sometimes you may hate one who is given more virtues by Allah" (H.Q.4:19).

The faithless Arabs looked upon the birth of female child as a curse. The evil practice of burying the excess female children were in vogue but Qur'an has strictly prohibited it as a cruel and unjust inhuman act. Qur'an attributes respectable position to women and he advises humanity to treat them kindly and respectfully. He has commanded that woman is the half of man. She will be told to enter Heaven through any way she likes, if she does Namaskar five times a day, practicing Vow in the month of Ramzan and she remains faithful and chaste to her husband.(Hades) 'Heaven is under the feet of mother.' It should be assured that all the rights of women are protected. "Those who do good to girls will escape from Hell." he who takes care of two female children until she is matured will be close to Me like two fingers in the next world. 'Divorce is legally permitted, but Allah does not like it'.

"Shall I show virtues to you? Behave most kindly to the divorced woman who goes from husband's house." 'He will be brought in Heaven who has a female child and does not bury the living child and does not scold or behave not differently' (Hades).

Almost all the gospels of the Prophet are against cruelty; especially cruelty towards women. The most virtuous man among you is he who do good to his wife' Prophet has said. No differences have been attributed to man and woman in their behavior towards Allah. Both of get good for good and evil for evil Qur'an says, "Sure, Allah has prepared forgiveness and great reward to those who, the man and woman who obey Allah, men and women who believe, sincere man and woman, patient man and woman, humble man and woman, charitable man and woman, man and woman who observe Vow, chaste man and woman man and woman who remember Allah" (H.Q.33:34).There is only one difference between them—Difference in their righteousness.

The faithless Arabs who thought woman had no human rights, stood against when they heard the declaration in the Quran "women have liabilities and respectable rights though men are a little high, Allah is reasonable and great" (H.Q.2:228).

The condition of widows was very deplorable in Arabia before the advent of Islam. Holy Qur'an has permitted remarriage. Divorce and marriage with another husband are not treated as bondage. It is converted as an agreement between equals. People should seriously think before separation. Either by the decision of one party or the by death marriage can be separated. With a view to lessen the contempt towards widows, the Prophet married many widows and took care of them.

A Muslim has no right to withhold the right of Muslim woman for education. The condition in western countries regarding freedom of women was very different. In western countries women themselves led struggles for the propriety right of women Islam has already permitted to Muslim women. The rights of Muslim women were allowed because of the efforts of men. Now men are trying to get full benefits out of Shariath.

Complaints are being raised by some people against practice of parents' selecting the husbands of girls. They say that girls should choose their husbands. This social law is not of Muslims alone. If the woman makes selection it means that the entire responsibility is hers. She may be inviting troubles. No Muslim would compel his daughter to live with the man she dislikes. See the ideals of Islam whenever think of liberation of woman. If they do not they will be misled But Islam's holy laws are dynamic. These are nobler than the laws of any other period. The rights of woman are increasing day by day along with their responsibilities. Islamic laws are equal to man and woman alike like the law of justice. Its aim is universal brotherhood. It contains brotherhood required for woman.

Even now some historians argue that the present Islamic system has reduced the status of India Muslim women. They consider it a credit to comment so. But the writers without preconceived ideas have agreed that the Prophet has brought many reforms in favor of women in Islam. The scandal against Prophet is really against truth. The development of nineteenth century carrying the heritage of an ancient culture has raised the status of women in Christian countries. But what is the status of women in Christian countries now.

Even in England a woman is not free from her husband. If a Muslim woman does not get the social standard of an English woman, Islamic system and orders may be challenged.

The great Prophet deserves credit and gratitude of the entire world for safeguarding the rights of Muslim women, when even western countries granted rights for women only by pressure from outside and inside. It was the place where the birth of a female child was regarded a sin. Even if He had not done any service to human race, he will be remembered as the most blessed man of humanity. On the basis of law there is equality between the rights of women in both countries. Until they are married they live in the care of parents.

To a considerable extent until she becomes mature, a Muslim woman is controlled by her father or his representative. But when she attains maturity she becomes an independent woman with all rights. She has right to her parents' property. Such a woman cannot be married to a man with out her complete consent. "Even the Sultan has no right to do so."

Marriage contract does not give any more freedom than the legal rights to a man on his wife. Like- wise a spend thrift husband has no freedom to destroy her savings not only that he cannot escape from punishment for his misbehavior or misconduct towards his wife. She can think and act of her own accord on matters of her property without waiting for her father's or husband's consent. She can conduct cases in public courts without the help of her husband or others. All the rights allowed to a man can be enjoyed by a woman even after coming to her husband's house from her house. She is guarded by all rights. It is not mere generosity or kindness. It is clearly stated in the Holy Text. Generally speaking the condition of a Muslim woman is not more ridiculous than that of a European woman. She has certain desirable status in certain scenes in life. However the backwardness existing among Muslim woman is not because of the laws made by great teachers of man kind.

Chapter 15
Polygamy

In certain stages of social development Polygamy becomes inevitable. It means a man's relation or union with many women. As a result of wars between clans and the shortage of men and the increase of women combined with the selfishness of rulers resulted in the evil and dirty custom of Polygamy, a practice which cannot be treated as decent.

It was an approved affair in all Eastern countries in ancient days. It had the hall mark of divinity as it existed among the landlords and kings. It became popular as a noble custom. Polygamy in two ways was prevalent among Hindus even from days of antiquity. There was no limit to the number of wives among the people of Babylonia Persia Syria and ancient Media. It was in vogue in Israel even before the time of Moses. A Jew husband can have any number of wives. Moses made no restriction on it. Later it was viewed in another angle. On the basis of husband's ability it was limited. Among Persians gifts were given by religion to those who have more number of wives.

Among the people of Athena the most civilized and cultured of the ancient western countries, wife was a commodity of exchange —to be sold and bought in the market. It was a commercial object to be transferred by death will of a man. She was regarded as a factor needed inevitably for producing children.

It grew up largely in Roman Empire until it was prohibited by Justinian's code of law. Except the first wife the others suffered a lot because of this. They underwent many tortures. They had no legal rights or protection of husband. They were mere slaves expected to be victims of man's greediness and cruelty. Their children were treated as illegal and exempted from the rights of father. They were really thrown outs in the society.

Ignoble and irregular marriages were not confined to the high class people only. Even priests, forgetting their celibacy, were engaged in many illegal and legal relations. History undisputably proves that Polygamy was not treated as a miserable thing until recently. St. Augustine did not see any sin or immorality in Polygamy. He declared that if it is a legally bound custom, is it not a crime. German reformers had approved it even in the sixteenth century. When there were no children or due to other urgent reasons they married another woman.

Whatever is the custom of the early Romans in the early days of the Republic, Polygamy was treated a custom or a legal affair. The courts in Rome had tried to divert the attention of the people to solve this issue. They succeeded in it. The laws framed by the kings of early 4th century, like Honorius and Arcadias prove that the emperor Constantine and his son were having many wives. In a stage the Emperor Valentine IInd declared that if the subjects are interested they had freedom for any number of wives. There is no record to show that either the Bishops or the Christian leaders made any objection to this law. All the Emperors and their successors had shown interest in Polygamy. And the people followed their footsteps.

This condition continued till the age of Athenian. The story of progress and development with centralized knowledge and experience of thirteen years ended with declaration of artificial laws in Justinian's notorious rule. They are called as Justinian's code of law. It has no direct connection with Christianity. His adviser was an Atheist. His declaration of prohibiting Polygamy made no impact among people. Law represents progressive thought its influence is confined only to some thinkers. It was an impracticable law to the rank and file.

Still the deplorable misunderstanding is that it was the Prophet who implemented Polygamy for the first time. He understood that it took vulgar forms not among Muslims only. Laws in Christian countries failed to eradicate this bad custom. It continued incessantly. All wives, except the first one, suffered a lot due to the cruelty of man.

There was no legal or religious control or limit in Arabia before Islam on relation with women. Islam made many restrictions and limit to better the society. It is alleged that Islam did not implement strict Monogamy. There are people who have questioned the Prophet-hood of Mohammed only because he had many wives. The domestic relation which lasted for twenty six years between Mohammed and Khadija is the model for Monogamy. It is not the one example alone. He has showed to us the noble model of Monogamy. Majority of people of the time were followers of Polygamy. The bad custom of treating women as animals existed in Arabia before the advent of Islam. It existed in many Christian countries even after Christ. It is a weakness of mind. In the interests of man and woman Islamic religion was restricting it.

The degeneration of moral scruples in Persia at the time of the Prophet was very miserable. No approved law was there for marriage if there was, it was completely neglected. There was no clear law about the number of wives one should marry in the Parse Texts. So Persians had many wives.

Apart from the system of marrying many wives, the ancient Arabs and Jews had many temporary and conditional relations with women on contract basis. She was only a commodity for sale. She was the unavoidable factor of her father's or husband's property. The widows of one man could be married either by his sons or others as the paternal share by tradition. So the sexual relations between husband's sons and step mothers were later prohibited by Islam. It was regarded as "Avanikahul mekth" (wicked marriage.)

Mohammed (S.A.) strictly prohibited conditional system of marriage that existed in Arabia. Temporary marriages were allowed in the initial stage. In the third year of Hijra it was prohibited. Prophet made many changes in the social conditions of women and safe guarded their rights. He made noteworthy changes in the status of women. He permitted rights and privileges which deserved credit and appreciation. Women were allowed rights and powers equal to men. Restriction was imposed on the number of marriages to be conducted at a time. It is the duty of man to ban Polygamy as it will spoil the reputation and status of women in the society. It is a note worthy thing that the permission given for Polygamy in the Qur'an has been confined within some legal and sensible limits. "you can marry up to four wives but if you cannot behave equally to all of them, you marry only one woman"(H.Q.4:3). There should be equality in house, clothes, other house hold affairs, love, emotion, and respect. The term 'Adel' means perfect equality. Emotional equality is not easily possible. So the instruction in Qur'an amounts to prohibition of Polygamy. Religious scholars studied that Qur'an laws really stand for Monogamy. Polygamy is against the progress, culture and teachings of the Prophet. This belief has deep roots in Muslim society.

Polygamy depends on circumstances. Some times it is meant for saving poor Muslim women from poverty and starvation. It has the role of a savior. If the statistics and statements are right the immoral practices in Western countries are born out of prohibition and it leads to Polygamy.

In that sense Polygamy is a favor permitted by Islam for the protection and care of both men and women. But it is Islam who implemented it for the first time in the world. Islam does not either persuade or compel to marry more than one woman. It tries to dissuade people from it. In peculiar circumstances Polygamy is permitted conditionally. The compulsion of situation is very important. It should be taken into account. That is why Islam is a perfect religion. The situations for Polygamy are natural. When a woman fails to do her duty as a wife due to pestilence or unable to conceive or not able to manage household affairs life is in peril. Then by chanting Thalak get separated from wife and marry another one. Or man should be ready to sacrifice everything for his wife. One of the ways is to be accepted.

In brief, Polygamy permitted by Islam, when practiced has many positive results. It saves the woman from becoming a harlot. Polygamy teaches the man responsibility of behavior towards women.

As the result of rapid changes and in thought and ideas, the need of Polygamy disappeared from and it is being neglected and uncared by people. The situation in early period has changed a lot in Islamic countries. Numbers of wives has become a burden and a social evil at present. It is a relief that Polygamy is not believed to be the teaching of the Prophet.

If once escaped from obsolete ideals and customs and gets freedom to think and act, every ruler of the Muslim country can abolish Polygamy by law. But it can be achieved only right understanding of Prophet's teachings and progress in in thought. When study his ideals in the right way, we know that Polygamy is losing its grip in the society. Shortly it will disappear completely.

Now the feelings against has become an emotional affair and a strong belief. Situations are being born among Muslim women in India to eradicate this social danger. Husbands who are going to marry should formally deny his freedom for divorce and it is included in the wedding letter as a condition. This system is a familiar one among Indian Muslims. Now ninety five percent of Muslims in India are the followers of Monogamy based on either belief or necessity. The learned and the wise men of other countries condemn it as a social evil. Now in Iran only a minority is after polygamy (20%). In a short while Polygamy will be declared as illegal and against Islamic laws, like slavery.

Chapter 16
Backwardness of Indian Muslims and Sachar Committee Report

The report submitted on the social and economical condition of Indian Muslim Community by the high power Committee with Rejoinder Sachar as the chairman is called Sachar Committee Report. It was reported in brief by Dr Said Safar Mohammad in Millie Gazette on 13th Dec 2006.

Neared Mishra said in the 'India Today' Dec 2006. "The social and educational condition of Indian Muslims is a surprise. But its solution is not a politically motivated reservation; its solution is to come from within the society itself."

India is second to Indonesia in the world of Muslim population. Perhaps in all the records so far collected except the case of prisoners, they are very backward. This Report regarding the condition of Indian Muslims comes out when the election works were going on in U. P. So it became of promises and required representation for the community a wonderful outburst of promises!

It is the second findings after the findings of Indian Sensus2001and National Sample Survey Organisation2004 a working committee employed by the Prime Minister to study the problems of the community also has pointed out the same issues in the report submitted to the Planning Commission. Former M.P. Shahabudeen said "This report is only a declaration of a political system, which separates Indian Muslim deliberately as a backward class; nothing new in the report except what we know."

While addressing the members of Minority Commission in Delhi the Prime Minister Man Mohan Singh placed the subject, 'necessary share dividends proportionate to the population of Muslims', for discussion. The Sachar Commission has already concentrated on the increasing gap between communities   regarding the job opportunities of Muslims and other backward classes in education, ownership of property, jobs in Govt: firms food on subsidy, hand pumps and tractor. Fifteen states, where Muslims live in plenty, have been considered for the study and from the records presented by the state Governments it was found out that the number of Muslims in Govt. jobs is very low.

Sachar has proved that Muslims do not represent proportionate to their population in Govt. jobs in each state. His findings as follows: 94.9% of Muslims live below poverty line, without getting free food. Only for 3.2% of Muslims get loan on low rate. There is no land for 2% even in villages. There are 15 lakhs of tractors in India. Out of it only 2.1% of Muslims have tractor. 11% of Muslims have tube wells. Muslims are not above 11% in Govt. jobs anywhere except Jammu Kashmir but national average is below 6%. The most deplorable record is from West Bengal where Communist party ruled for thirty years. 25% of the population in West Bengal is Muslims. But they represent only 4.2% in Govt. jobs. In public sectors there are no Muslims, only 5% is in the department of Law and Justice. The Commission failed to find out the Muslim representation in top Govt. jobs.

The official Gazette declared in the year 2005 March in the Prime Ministers office said that there is no authentic information about the social, educational and economic condition of Muslim community in India. Scarcity of information will affect planning, policy formation and the schemes to be finished time bound. So it was forced to conduct a deep survey about the condition of Muslims in education. So it collected information from state and central representatives. According to it this Committee has to probe deep in to the economic condition of Muslims in different states. How much is their labor representation in public and private sector? Whether they are proportionally represented in all states? Is this proportion equal in all states? Or what are the objections? The Committee has to find out from the total OBC the OBC of Muslim community. Whether Muslim O.B.C. is included in the list of Backward communities of the state and central Governments. How much is the representation of Muslims in central Government's Central Labor

Representation? Have they got access like the other communities? What is the position of public enterprises (schools, Basic health – centers etc.) in places where Muslim population is very high. The Committee has to find out where the Government should interfere to raise the standard of life of the Muslims

This report submitted to the Prime Minister in 2006 Nov17th was placed before the Parliament. This report had 12 chapters. First chapter is preface General views and observations of got from the public people in the states with thick Muslim population placed in the Round Table Conference organized in Delhi, is in the second chapter. The committee has visited 13 states where Muslim population is very high. Third chapter discusses the population its distribution and condition of Health. The next chapters discuss the condition of education.

Contents

1 Factors

2 Important findings in the report

3 Remove the old and general notions

4 The gist of recommendation

5 Reactions on the findings of the Committee

1)15 Instructions for the welfare of minorities

2) Serve- Shisha Abeyance

3) Improve the conditions of girls of Minority Communities

4) Find out the Districts where Muslims are in majority

5) Criticism

6) Responses of organizations and Political Parties

7) Submit for consideration

8) Additions

Factors

In this Committee there were seven members including Four Muslim women. The head was Rejoinder Sachar. Sayid Hamid, Dr.T.K.Ummen, M.A.Basith, Dr.Akthar Majeed, Dr.Abusalif Sharif, Dr.RakeshBasanth were members. Sayid Safar Mohammad was appointed by the Prime Minister for special duty.

Women's organization alleged that there is no woman representation in the Committee. When visited all the states half day discussion was made with women organization. Women social workers had participated in all the meetings and expressed their suggestions in the matter. In the meetings it was emphasized about the needs of education, conveniences in Medical field, and Nursery. A one day meeting was conducted in Delhi where women all over India took part.

Findings in the Report

Sachar Committee discussed in detail the statistics collected from Indian Minority Commission, Banks, Government Committees and different State Committees.

1) According to this report the condition of Muslim Minority is better than that of Scheduled Castes and Scheduled Tribes and worse than the other Back ward communities. Like wise the condition of Muslim Dalit category is very pitiable. It is found out that literacy of Muslim is below the National proportion. There is conspicuous difference regarding literacy in urban areas comparing to other communities. It is also found out that Twenty five percent of Muslim children do not go to schools or they stop it before completing.

2) Muslim parents show aversion to the main stream of Education or they do not send children to schools. To Muslim children convenience to reach school was very less.

3) Financial aid and social security would have been given to beedy-laborers, Tailors and Mechanics.

In the Technical and Administrative fields the participation of Muslim is very meager.

4) Only 2/3 of the sum of Bank Loan distributed to the Other Backward communities was given to Muslims In certain contexts it was only just half. The loan scheme of Reserve Bank, as per the Prime Minister's 15 item programs was useful more to the other communities than the Muslims. Since majority of Muslims are self employed, the lacking of Bank loan created inconvenience. It made the situation of Muslims worse.

5) The lack of availability of basic requirements proportionate to the population of Muslims is a negative factor. In Muslim populated villages sub roads and local bus stops are very rare.

6) Muslims families can spend only an amount below 500 Rs in urban areas.

7) Representation of Muslims in I.A.S. is only 3%, in I.F.S. 1.8% and in I.P.S 4%.

8) Muslims have only 4.5% representation in Indian Railway Service. In that 98.7% of people are employed in low posts. In Banks and Universities their representation is very less. Muslims are only 6% in the post of Police, in the Health Department, 4.4% and in the Transport Department 6.5%.

The opportunities that came along with Economic growth could not be utilized because of the lack of education. The right for education is a fundamental right. This report throws light upon the difficulties suffered by Muslims in the absence of education. They have two kinds of inconveniences –low and education without quality. As per the standard of education, their suffering also increased. 25% of Muslim children in between 6 to 14 years had not got school education, or they gave up it. As far as higher education is concerned, Muslim graduates are below 4% It is only 7% of National average. They are 20 years old or above it. In the case of Post-Graduation Muslim is only one out of twenty.

9) Financial Aid to the efficient working of Maul Ana Azad Education Foundation should be raised up to Rs. 1000 cr. Details of this scheme has not been clearly published. Even though Muslim participation is less in Administrative Committees, new members should also take part in the decision making meetings.

10) The differences show that there is clear distinction between Hindu O.B.C and Muslim O.B.C. It is seen in the job proportion too. In the government and private sectors Muslim participation is very low comparing to the Hindu O.B.C.

11) The registered wakaf-board has property of 6,00,000 lakhs and savings of Rs.6,000 Cr.

Eradicate mechanical thoughts

Sachar Committee was beneficial to expose the misunderstandings stated by right social organizations as a part of their political propaganda.

1) Only 4% of Muslim students go to school. The schools are miles beyond. Note that they do not give importance to Madrasa education.

2) 200 Lakhs of Muslims are using modern methods to avoid pregnancy. So there is considerable decrease in Muslim population. The dangerous propaganda, that Muslims try to increase population by increasing birth rate, is stopped. It is also said that it is the result of Muslim conspiracy after 1947.

3) Muslims complain that they are scandalized in two ways. Firstly they are stamped as Anti National people and supporters of Anti Nationalism. Sachar Committee revealed that Muslims as a whole are not resorted to Anti National activities.

Sachar Commission was brave enough to state frankly that all the Muslims have been stamped as antinational people though only a few was engaged in Anti National Activities. So the Commission says that Muslims are bound to prove that they are neither Anti National or Terrorists. This preconceived notion adversely affects the social and economical conditions of the Muslims. This is perhaps the most important allegation they confront. Unemployment, poverty and shortage of educational opportunities are the main problems all Indians face. Even after 60 years of independent rule in India, Muslims and other communities remain as of old. That means, real problems have not yet been solved.

A social revolt is necessary for growing unity among the people in their basic issues. When racial struggles stood uncompromising in their views, and unity existed among all religions and castes, the attempts of the Government to divide the people did not succeed. The Armed Revolution of Telungana is a good experience and a witness. The same thing happened among the Weavers in Bombay. Muslims should organize as one and fight for democratic rights and attempts should be made to create unity among Muslims. That means another democratic revolution. The way to escape from is only by making deep rooted changes in the social and educational conditions of the majority of people. It can be done only by the combined efforts of people at large.

Sachar commission had observed that Muslim's burden of life is doubled. In 1978 Janatha Party Government appointed a Minority

commission. In 1980 Congress Government made another committee, leaving aside the former one. But the commission did not present
the report before the people. In 1995 another report regarding the
repersentation of Muslims in Police and Parliamentary Services, was
submitted. In 1996 Planning commission submitted some instructions.
All these commissions brought out the miserable condititon of Muslims and solutions were also suggested. But nothing happened as expected.

Things as such, a question may arise. The Government had all
records in its custody. So why a new commission was appointed? Why
pretend that the Government came to know of the sad plight only
now? And why advise that the progress should reach the Muslims first?

The false propaganda that Muslims are world terrorists and anti-
nationalists began by the middle of 1980. Those who propagate so,
influence the Government and spread scandals and malice against the
Muslim community. On the other side some others, pretending to be
protectors of Muslims try by all means to stamp Muslims as racialists.
Those who claim as secularists accuse that Muslims are being gratified
by the Government. But the truth is that both the parties depict Muslims as Terrorists; it is nothing but sadism. The propaganda that Muslims are anti-nationalists and the planned-attempts of Hindu Racialists
are not accidental. It is the result of New Liberal policy of World Bank
and International money savings. It is the part of Government's Policy
divde and rule. When people are separated so the objections of the
people against modernization would become weak or the issues would
remain unsolved. An examination of even silly thing in the past days
would make it clear.

When one party considers Babar - I - Masjid and Rama temple
as agenda of the ruling government was helping those who sent this
message in each house. Though there were evidences that Babar-I-
Masjid would be demolished, ruling party stood a silent witness until it
collapsed. It was followed by homicide in many places. But political
parties were anxious to put all the blame of bomb explosion on the
Muslim Terrorists. Even though many Commissions concluded that
Muslims have no connection with Gothra Incident a massacre took
place in Gujarat. It was a revolt with political support. No actions have
been taken against the criminals.

Important recommendations

Sachar Committee has put forward some suggestions for changing the deplorable state of Muslims. The betterment of Minority and the strengthening of would increase their progress and patriotism.

Recommendations

1) Equality of rights and opportunities would be assured. Make preparations for eradicating discrimination

2) Establish National Data Bank and collect details of religion and castes

3) Set up An Independent Income Assessment Committee and a new system to inform them about the development results among the people

4) A Committee for ensuring equal opportunity for all and solve the grievances of the losers of chances

5) Assess the boundaries and solve the complaints of Reservation Constituencies

6) Give equal chances to people in Education House construction Private sectors and Government

7) Assess the cost of school Text books and implement it

8) Communal Student Representation should be assured in Colleges and Universities

9) Hostel accommodations to be arranged for students of Minority classes. Take steps according to priority

10) Committee recommended for giving Bank loans in Muslim Majority places

11) Formation of policy for backward classes or Muslims to be sharers in Bank transactions

12) Muslims would have representation in Boards and Interviews

13) Give financial and other aids to labor zones where Muslims have concentrated

14) Sachar Committee does not instruct Reservation. The constitutional favors given to Minority communities among Hindus should be given to the Muslims too

Reactions and actions followed in 15 items of Minority welfare activities.

Indian Prime Minister implemented 15 items of programs for the betterment of Minority Community.

As per new programs educational chances for the Minorities increased. Their role in financial matters was confirmed. Job opportunities and Standard of life were improved. It tried to reduce communal disharmony and violence among the people.

Sarva Shisha Abeyance

It is a National scheme for giving Education for all. That means, implement time bound qualitative education for children from six years to Fourteen years. The Government had conducted survey through Census, District Information System for Education (DISE) in order to find help the children of Minority Muslim Community. It was done under Serve Shisha abeyance (SSA). The construction of schools were assured in the areas where the Minorities are thickly populated. In the year 2005-2006 4,624 primary schools were sanctioned. 31,702 centres for education were also granted. In these Districts 6,918 new Primary and Upper Primary schools were sanctioned in the year 2006-2007. Later 32,250 Education centers were startedand for 11.25 lakhs of children parallel education was confirmed. Madrasas and Maktabs came under S.S.A. The Madrasas joined to the State Madrasa Board were given some conditional aids given to SSA schools. 8,309 Madrasas got this aid.

Accommodations set up for children of Minority Community

Distributed freely text books for children of Minority Community of First to Eight classes. Urdu Text books were supplied to Urdu medium students. Urdu is declared as a language. According to censes in 1981, 93 Districts have been declared as centers of Importance. The centers in Bihar, U.P, West Bengal and Assam are given more attention. Out of 1,180 Kasturba Gandhi Children School, it was ordered to set up 210 schools in Minority zones. On 31-3-2006, 1,430 girls were admitted in Kasturba Gandhi children School. Apart from it, attention had been drawn to 93 Districts having 20% Muslim population as per the census in 1981. Sarva Shisha Abeyance Scheme was implemented there in the years 2005-2006 and 2006-2007.

The Sachar Report was placed on the table. After that Muslim Members of Parliament submitted a report of their intentions to the Human Resources Development Minister Arjun Singh. The requirements stated in the list are, I.I.T., I.M.S. 5,000 Schools, 2 lakhs of Scholarships and more campuses of All egad Muslim University all over India. This list was prepared as the result of discussions made by Ten Muslim M.Ps who met in the Islamic cultural center. The minister I.H.R.D Ali Ashraf Fatimid and other top level officers were present in the meeting.

Fatimid the head of High Power Committee of the H. R.Minister spoke to the Indian Express: 'An open discussion' was made with Members of Parliament in matters from the Primary and Higher Education. They had many novel ideas. They demanded 2,000 Central Schools for Muslim Children 1,000 to boys and 1,000 to girls.

The Members of Parliament demanded to set up 3,000 Residential Schools in the model of Kasturba Gandhi Children School, for girls as the primary education of girls is very poor. And also demanded to set up Universities all through India in the model of Maul Ana Azad National Urdu University. They also wanted 2 lakhs Scholarships for Muslim students in the Higher Education Level. It would create more chances for the students.

Thus the recommendations of the Sachar Committee implemented free and time bound education in the fields of education. School Text books were made to satisfy the interests of the community. Government schools with high quality of standard were set up in the areas where Muslim girls lived in majority.

It was decided to teach Urdu as optional language in the primary schools of areas where people speak Urdu. Thus the policies of the Government make it clear that the Government moves according to the report of the Sachar Committee.

■

Texts referred

1) Islamic Darsanam (Kerala Language Institute approved by Kerala and Calicut University.

2) Islamika Samskara (Cultural side of Islam) Trans: K. Hussan.

3) Islaminte Atmave (Spirit of Islam), Sayyid Amir Ali. Trans: A.Kochunni

4) Hajj-Alisariathi Trans:-Kalim(I.P.H.)

5) Qur'an Laliyha saram-Shaik Mohammad Karakkunnu, Vanidas, Elayavooru.

6) Sahihul Bukhari-Mohammad Bukhari. Trans: C.N.Ahammad Maulavi.

7) Islam Rajamargam-Alija Ali Essath Begovich Trans: N.P.Mohammad.

8) Islam, Oru Samagra Patanam-C.N.Ahammad Maulavi.

www.ingramcontent.com/pod-product-compliance
Lightning Source LLC
Chambersburg PA
CBHW051356280526
45784CB00007B/2983